Praise for The Game of Life

"The secret of her success was that she was always herself . . . colloquial, informal, friendly, and humorous. She herself was very spiritual . . . and taught by familiar, practical, and everyday examples."

—Emmet Fox, author of *The Sermon on the Mount*

"By studying and practicing the principles laid down in this book, one may find prosperity, solve problems, have better health, achieve personal relations—in a word, win the game of life."

—Norman Vincent Peale,
author of *The Power of Positive Thinking*

"*The Game of Life and How to Play It*, by Florence Scovel Shinn, helped me crystallize my own thinking and moved me forward on the path to where I am today."

—Louise Hay, author of *You Can Heal Your Life*

The Game
of Life
and How to
Play It

The Game
of Life
and How to
Play It

Florence Scovel Shinn
INCLUDES EXPANDED STUDY GUIDE BY CHRIS GENTRY

HAMPTON ROADS

Cover design by Howard Grossman

Hampton Roads Publishing Company, Inc.
Charlottesville, VA 22906
Distributed by Red Wheel/Weiser, LLC
www.redwheelweiser.com
Sign up for our newsletter and special offers by going to
www.redwheelweiser.com/newsletter.

ISBN: 978-1-64297-047-0
Library of Congress Cataloging-in-Publication Data

Names: Shinn, Florence Scovel, 1871-1940, author. | Gentry, Chris, 1965-
   writer of added commentary.
Title: The game of life and how to play it / Florence Scovel Shinn ; with
   additional material by Chris Gentry ; foreword by Laura Berman Fortgang.
Description: Newburyport, MA : Weiser Books, 2023. | Summary: "'Most people
   consider life a battle. It's not a battle. . . . It's a game. And like
   most games, it can't be played successfully without understanding the
   rules.' In a clear and accessible manner, this book explores the six key
   rules for the game of life, providing to readers a user's manual for
   making informed decisions and fully embracing a life of success and
   happiness. Also included are study questions, meditations, and action
   items"-- Provided by publisher.
Identifiers: LCCN 2022054237 | ISBN 9781642970470 (trade paperback) | ISBN
   9781612834863 (kindle edition)
Subjects: LCSH: Success--Psychological aspects. | New Thought. |
   Spirituality. | Conduct of life. | BISAC: BODY, MIND & SPIRIT / New
   Thought | SELF-HELP / Personal Growth / Happiness
Classification: LCC BF637.S8 S517 2023 | DDC 158.1--dc23/eng/20221212
LC record available at https://lccn.loc.gov/2022054237

Printed in the United States of America
IBI
10 9 8 7 6 5 4 3 2 1

Contents

Foreword

Human nature and its inherited traditions have made us very serious and weighed down by our circumstances. Life would be so much more fun if we could think of it as a game. It may seem preposterous to some, but Florence Scovel Shinn knew early on the secrets that could unlock a joyful existence, one where we truly feel we are cooperating with the organizing forces of life and are able to have what we want. And now, Chris Gentry has funneled Shinn's theories and stories into a concrete set of exercises that will help you weave her teachings deep into the fabric of your life and make them work for you.

The "game" of life hasn't changed much, but people have evolved. I think they are now, more then ever, ready to hear what Shinn knew so many years ago. It's our most organic and essential qualities that need to be honed so life can feel like a game.

As I revisited this classic book, I was struck anew by certain areas of interest that coincidentally stacked up to spell L-I-F-E: Love, Intuition, Fear, and Expectation.

Love

The act of reading this book and taking on Shinn's teachings is an act of love. To stop the torture of how you approach things now and turn your thinking over to kinder thoughts—and, therefore, actions—is a milestone in your spiritual growth. Operating in this way is kinder to your soul, and all those around you will benefit as well.

You'll find life to be kinder when you are kinder to yourself. The voice in your head will change as you give it heed or not. Love it back and calm it. When it wants to attack others, talk it out of its meanness. Love yourself out of every problem by sending love to all those involved. Having trouble with your boss? Send them love. Arguing with your sibling? Send them love. No matter how disdainful another's actions might be, send them love. Love will ease the way.

Intuition

Florence says that IN-tuition means being taught from within. I say that intuition is the most important 21st century life skill we can nurture. We are wired to be our own rudder, but for dozens of decades we've allowed outside sources to decide our lives.

In a world where the rules of work, government, religion, environment, and every system we've come to rely on are in constant flux, there is only one ruling factor to decision-making in your life: You. You may look to God or some other source for guidance, but ultimately trusting yourself (your intuition) is paramount to navigating what lies ahead.

I work with people every day who are excavating their way to clarity on their career and their life path, and they often ask me if they are crazy to listen to what they want most and what their intuition is telling them. The answer, of course, is no. Especially when those around them are asking if they are crazy to give up their job or consider something illogical, I tell them: "If everyone thinks you're crazy, you're on the right track! Keep going!"

Fear

Fear is the eternal enemy to living the life we most desire, its voice so powerful we believe it above any other authority. Shinn says: "Fear is inverted faith." We have faith in evil instead of good. She asks us to "wish without worrying," which is essential to succeeding in the Game of Life. It's easy to believe and have faith for a while. However, as the days go on, and the timeline we had hoped for evaporates into an excuse to become hopeless, we are being asked to take on a whole other skill set.

The belief that the universe has our back and truly wants what is good for us has to be felt with every fiber of your body and soul (the subconscious mind, according to Shinn) to succeed at the Game of Life. This depth of trust directly correlates to our expectations.

Expectation

I was a born worrier. Maybe it's just part of being the oldest child, or maybe it's a product of a vivid imagination, but I learned to worry as a way to feel safe. Ironically, imagining the worst-case scenario and then coming up with a solution to it enabled me to put the fear aside like an item crossed off a checklist.

"Done. I'm prepared, so no need to worry," I would think.

Over the years, as I studied metaphysics and read books like this one, I've worked hard to stop preparing for the worst altogether and just expect the best.

We are afraid to expect the best because perhaps we don't want to be naïve or get caught unprepared if something bad were to happen. Maybe we even feel ashamed to think there's hubris in ignoring the pitfalls (thus, my own 'prepare for the worst, but expect the best' philosophy). I've allowed that to change, and I hope you will too. As per Shinn, our words and our thoughts are only meant to "heal, bless, and prosper." We are to live fully expectant of the results we desire. I've tried it, and I highly recommend it. It feels so good. It creates a high vibration in your being, and we know that is the prerequisite for a high-quality life. Being fully expectant of great things harms no one.

Over all these years, the Game of Life hasn't changed; but this book is a game-changer. Expect it to change you and your life for the best.

—*Laura Berman Fortgang*

Introduction

This edition of *The Game of Life and How to Play It* contains the complete and original text, exactly as it was originally published in 1925. Since its publication, it has influenced millions. Why? I believe it is because author Florence Scovel Shinn was a master at taking profound spiritual concepts and making them accessible and practical.

I was first given a copy of *The Game of Life* by a friend who insisted this book had changed her life, and that it could do the same for me. As I held that copy in my hands, I remember thinking that this slim little book seemed too simple and too short to contain any "real" ideas that could work for me. And I also felt that since it had been published many years before I was born, the ideas were probably outdated. However, once I began reading, I quickly changed my mind. Here was a guide to life that was easy to understand and incredibly motivating, and it contained practical ideas that I could implement immediately—and I did. The more I used the ideas in *The Game of Life*, the more success I had in every area. I've read this book many times over the years, and I began teaching classes on it about a decade ago. It continues to inspire me to live my life more fully, and more joyfully, and I've seen firsthand how it positively and powerfully affects the lives of those in my classes.

A couple quick notes before you read *The Game of Life*. It was published in 1925, before a more gender-neutral language was the norm. I've decided to keep the language as is in this edition, not wanting to change the book from the way it was originally intended by the author. However, it is not difficult to translate her message for either gender as you read through the text—the ideas expressed may often use masculine pronouns, but the ideas themselves obviously have no gender and will work for anyone who uses them consciously.

Another tip—it can be more powerful to study this book slowly, rather than give in to the temptation of reading it all in one sitting. Despite its slender size, each chapter is packed with principles and suggestions that require more than a moment's consideration. What I do, and what I teach others to do, is read one chapter each week, for ten weeks. Since the chapters are short, each one can be read from start to finish every day for a week, or divided up into small sections to read every day.

To further help readers, at the end of each chapter I've included reflection questions to help you digest the material and perhaps shine a light on some of the most important ideas. I've also included exercises to help you incorporate the ideas into your life immediately. After all, knowledge isn't useful unless we use it to make our lives better. You'll notice inspirational quotes appear throughout the chapters as well. This is to provide further bite-sized wisdom that can give you aha moments.

Finally, the book concludes with two very special appendixes based on my many years of teaching this material. The first appendix contains a very simple exercise that can help you to discover and choose goals that will enhance and enlarge your life. Sometimes we can feel rudderless, not knowing where we are going; however, if we aren't moving toward anything in life, we can feel directionless and lost. When we clearly define what we want in life, we then have a "North Star" that we can move toward each and every day.

Because I've found that studying this book with another person, or a small group of people, is even more powerful than reading it alone, I've included a second appendix which contains some very simple guides to forming a reading group. As Shinn points out, when two or more people come together to discover and practice these powerful principles, the results are magnified for all involved. Plus, studying with other people makes the process more fun.

My final piece of advice is this: Don't just read this book. Devour it. Use it. Test it. Write in the margins, highlight your favorite sentences, write your own affirmations. In other words, make this book not just a book, but rather a guide for life—*your* life! If something sounds too simple or too good to be true, try it out earnestly and wholeheartedly and see if it works for you. Enter into this book with a spirit of openness, and let it take you on a very important journey—the journey to your success!

—*Chris Gentry*

THE COMPLETE

GAME

OF

LIFE

AND HOW TO

PLAY

IT

The Game of Life

Most people consider life a battle, but life is not a battle, it is a game.

It is a game, however, which cannot be played successfully without the knowledge of spiritual law, and the Old and the New Testaments give the rules of the game with wonderful clearness. Jesus Christ taught that it was a great game of *Giving and Receiving*.

"Whatsoever a man soweth that shall he also reap." This means that whatever man sends out in word or deed, will return to him: what he gives, he will receive.

If he gives hate, he will receive hate; if he gives love, he will receive love; if he gives criticism, he will receive criticism; if he lies he will be lied to; if he cheats he will be cheated. We are taught also, that the imaging faculty plays a leading part in the game of life.

"Keep thy heart (or imagination) with all diligence, for out of it are the issues of life." (Prov. 4:23.)

This means that what man images, sooner or later externalizes in his affairs. I know of a man who feared a certain disease. It was a very rare disease and difficult to get, but he pictured it continually and read about it until it manifested in his body, and he died, the victim of distorted imagination.

So we see, to play successfully the game of life, we must train the imaging faculty. A person with an imaging faculty trained to image only good, brings into his life "every righteous desire of his heart"—health, wealth, love, friends, perfect self-expression, his highest ideals.

The imagination has been called, *"The Scissors of The Mind,"* and it is ever cutting, cutting, day by day, the pictures man sees there, and sooner or later he meets his own creations in his outer world. To train the imagination successfully, man must understand the workings of his mind. The Greeks said: "Know Thyself."

> "Take care of each moment and you will take care of all time."
>
> —Buddha

There are three departments of the mind, the *subconscious, conscious and superconscious.* The subconscious, is simply power, without direction. It is like steam or electricity, and it does what it is directed to do; it has no power of induction.

Whatever man feels deeply or images clearly, is impressed upon the subconscious mind, and carried out in minutest detail.

For example: a woman I know, when a child, always "made believe" she was a widow. She "dressed up" in black clothes and wore a long black veil, and people thought she was very clever and amusing. She grew up and married a man with whom she was deeply in love. In a short time he died and she wore black and a sweeping veil for many years. The picture of herself as a widow was impressed upon the subconscious mind, and in due time worked itself out, regardless of the havoc created.

The conscious mind has been called mortal or carnal mind.

It is the human mind and sees life as it *appears to be*. It sees death, disaster, sickness, poverty and limitation of every kind, and it impresses the subconscious.

The *superconscious* mind is the God Mind within each man, and is the realm of perfect ideas.

In it, is the *"perfect pattern"* spoken of by Plato, *The Divine Design;* for there is a *Divine Design* for each person.

"There is a place that you are to fill and no one else can fill, something you are to do, which no one else can do."

There is a perfect picture of this in the *superconscious mind*. It usually flashes across the conscious as an unattainable ideal— "something too good to be true."

In reality it is man's true destiny (or destination) flashed to him from the Infinite Intelligence which is *within himself*.

Many people, however, are in ignorance of their true destinies and are striving for things and situations which do not belong to them, and would only bring failure and dissatisfaction if attained.

For example: A woman came to me and asked me to "speak the word" that she would marry a certain man with whom she was very much in love. (She called him A. B.)

I replied that this would be a violation of spiritual law, but that I would speak the word for the right man, the "divine selection," the man who belonged to her by divine right.

I added, "If A. B. is the right man you can't lose him, and if he isn't, you will receive his equivalent." She saw A. B. frequently but no headway was made in their friendship. One evening she called, and said, "Do you know, for the last week, A. B. hasn't seemed so wonderful to me." I replied, "Maybe he is not the divine selection—another man may be the right one." Soon after that, she met another man who fell in love with her at once, and who said she was his ideal. In fact, he said all the things that she had always wished A. B. would say to her.

She remarked, "It was quite uncanny."

She soon returned his love, and lost all interest in A. B.

This shows the law of substitution. A right idea was substituted for a wrong one, therefore there was no loss or sacrifice involved.

"With God all things are possible."
—Matthew 19:26

. . . .

Jesus Christ said, "Seek ye first the kingdom of God and his righteousness; and all these things shall be added unto you," and he said the Kingdom *was within man*.

The Kingdom is the realm of *right ideas*, or the divine pattern.

Jesus Christ taught that man's words played a leading part in the game of life. "By your words ye are justified and by your words ye are condemned."

Many people have brought disaster into their lives through idle words.

For example: A woman once asked me why her life was now one of poverty and of limitation. Formerly she had a home, was surrounded by beautiful things and had plenty of money. We found she had often tired of the management of her home, and had said repeatedly, "I'm sick and tired of things—I wish I lived in a trunk," and she added: "Today I am living in that trunk." She had spoken herself into a trunk. The subconscious mind has no sense of humor and people often joke themselves into unhappy experiences.

For example: A woman who had a great deal of money, joked continually about "getting ready for the poorhouse."

In a few years she was almost destitute, having impressed the subconscious mind with a picture of lack and limitation.

Fortunately the law works both ways, and a situation of lack may be changed to one of plenty.

For example: A woman came to me one hot summer's day for a "treatment" for prosperity. She was worn out, dejected and discouraged. She said she possessed just eight dollars in the world. I said, "Good, we'll bless the eight dollars and multiply them as Jesus Christ multiplied the loaves and fishes," for He taught that *every man* had the power to bless and to multiply, to heal and to prosper.

She said, "What shall I do next?"

I replied, "Follow intuition. Have you a 'hunch' to do anything, or to go anywhere?" Intuition means, intuition, or to be taught from within. It is man's unerring guide, and I will deal more fully with its laws in a following chapter.

> "Desire is God tapping at the door of your mind, trying to give you greater good."
>
> —Catherine Ponder

The woman replied: "I don't know—I seem to have a 'hunch' to go home; I've just enough money for carfare." Her home was in a distant city and was one of lack and limitation, and the reasoning mind (or intellect) would have said: "Stay in New York and get work and make some money." I replied, "Then go home—never violate a hunch." I spoke the following words for her: *Infinite Spirit open the way for great abundance for _____. She is an irresistible magnet for all that belongs to her by divine right."* I told her to repeat it continually also. She left for home immediately. In calling on a woman one day, she linked up with an old friend of her family.

Through this friend, she received thousands of dollars in a most miraculous way. She has said to me often, "Tell people about the woman who came to you with eight dollars and a hunch."

There is always *plenty on man's pathway*; but it can only be *brought into manifestation* through desire, faith or the spoken word. Jesus Christ brought out clearly that man must make the *first move*.

Ask, and it shall be given you, seek, and ye shall find, knock, and it shall be opened unto you. (Mat. 7:7).

In the Scriptures we read:

"Concerning the works of my hands, command ye me."

Infinite Intelligence, God, is ever ready to carry out man's smallest or greatest demands.

Every desire, uttered or unexpressed, is a demand. We are often startled by having a wish suddenly fulfilled.

For example: One Easter, having seen many beautiful rose-trees in the florists' windows, I wished I would receive one, and for an instant saw it mentally being carried in the door.

Easter came, and with it a beautiful rose-tree. I thanked my friend the following day, and told her it was just what I had wanted.

She replied, "I didn't send you a rose-tree, I sent you lilies!"

The man had mixed the order, and sent me a rose-tree simply because I had started the law in action, and *I had to have a rose-tree*.

> "Today I recognize the abundance of life. I
> animate everything in my experience with this
> idea."
>
> —Ernest Holmes

Nothing stands between man and his highest ideals and every desire of his heart, but doubt and fear. When man can "wish without worrying," every desire will be instantly fulfilled.

I will explain more fully in a following chapter the scientific reason for this and how fear must be erased from the consciousness. It is man's only enemy—fear of lack, fear of failure, fear of sickness, fear of loss and a feeling of *insecurity on some plane*. Jesus Christ said: "Why are ye fearful, oh ye of little faith?" (Mat. 8:26). So we can see we must substitute faith for fear, for fear is only inverted faith; it is faith in evil instead of good.

The object of the game of life is to see clearly one's good and to obliterate all mental pictures of evil. This must be done by impressing the subconscious mind with a realization of good. A very brilliant man, who has attained great success, told me he had suddenly erased all fear from his consciousness by reading a sign which hung in a room. He saw printed, in large letters this statement—"*Why worry, it will probably never happen.*" These words were stamped indelibly upon his subconscious mind, and he has now a firm conviction that only good can come into his life, therefore only *good can manifest*.

In the following chapter I will deal with the different methods of impressing the subconscious mind. It is man's faithful servant but one must be careful to give it the right orders. Man has ever a silent listener at his side—his subconscious mind.

Every thought, every word is impressed upon it and carried out in amazing detail. It is like a singer making a record on the sensitive disc of the phonographic plate. Every note and tone of the singer's voice is registered. If he coughs or hesitates, it is registered also. So let us break all the old bad records in the subconscious mind, the records of our lives which we do not wish to keep, and make new and beautiful ones.

Speak these words aloud, with power and conviction: "I now smash and demolish (by my spoken word) every untrue record in my subconscious mind. They shall return to the dust-heap of their native nothingness, for they came from my own vain imaginings. I now make my perfect records through the Christ within—The records of *Health, Wealth, Love and perfect self-Expression.*" This is the square of life, *The Game completed.*

In the following chapters, I will show how man can *change* his *conditions by changing his words.* Any man who does not know the power of the word, is behind the times.

"Death and Life are in the power of the tongue." (Prov. 18:21.)

REFLECT . . . .

1. If life is a "great game of Giving and Receiving" (p. 1), do you think you are in balance with both giving to life and receiving from life? If not, where are you out of balance? And why?

2. "Many people . . . are in ignorance of their true destinies and are striving for things and situations which do not belong to them, and would only bring failure and dissatisfaction if attained" (p. 4).

   Have you, or anyone you know, had this experience? If so, what happened?

3. Which of the stories in this chapter do you relate to most? Why? What did you learn from it?

TAKE YOUR TURN . . . .

1. You must follow your intuition. Do you have a "hunch" for next steps in your life? If so, what is your hunch telling you to do?

2. Look at this hunch, and if possible immediately take the first step toward making it happen, before it loses energy. Never delay acting on a hunch until tomorrow.

3. Pick one of the affirmations or positive statements from this chapter. Write it down on a small piece of paper or sticky note, and repeat it one hundred times each day for a week. Notice all the ways (big or small) your life mirrors this positive idea.

The Law of Prosperity

"*Yea, the Almighty shall be thy defense and thou shalt have plenty of silver.*"

One of the greatest messages given to the race through the scriptures is that God is man's supply and that man can release, *through his spoken word*, all that belongs to him by divine right. He must, however, have *perfect faith in his spoken word*.

Isaiah said, "My word shall not return unto me void, but shall accomplish that where unto it is sent." We know now, that words and thoughts are a tremendous vibratory force, ever moulding man's body and affairs.

A woman came to me in great distress and said she was to be sued on the fifteenth of the month for three thousand dollars. She knew no way of getting the money and was in despair.

I told her God was her supply, and *that there is a supply for every demand*.

So I spoke the word! I gave thanks that the woman would receive three thousand dollars at the right time in the right way. I told her she must have perfect faith, and act her *perfect faith*. The fifteenth came but no money had materialized.

She called me on the 'phone and asked what she was to do.

I replied, "It is Saturday, so they won't sue you today. Your part is to act rich, thereby showing perfect faith that you will receive it by Monday." She asked me to lunch with her to keep up her courage. When I joined her at a restaurant, I said, "This is no time to economize. Order an expensive luncheon, act as if you have already received the three thousand dollars."

"All things whatsoever ye ask in prayer, *believing*, ye shall receive." "You must act as if you *had already received*." The next morning she called me on the 'phone and asked me to stay with her during the day. I said "No, you are divinely protected and God is never too late."

In the evening she 'phoned again, greatly excited and said, "My dear, a miracle has happened! I was sitting in my room this morning, when the doorbell rang. I said to the maid: 'Don't let anyone in.' The maid however, looked out the window and said, 'It's your cousin with the long white beard.'

So I said, 'Call him back. I would like to see him.' He was just turning the corner, when he heard the maid's voice, and *he came back*.

He talked for about an hour, and just as he was leaving he said, 'Oh, by the way, how are finances?'

I told him I needed the money, and he said, 'Why, my dear, I will give you three thousand dollars the first of the month.'

I didn't like to tell him I was going to be sued. What shall I do? I won't *receive it till* the first of the month, and I must have it tomorrow." I said, "I'll keep on 'treating.'"

I said, "Spirit is never too late. I give thanks she has received the money on the invisible plane and that it manifests on time." The next morning her cousin called her up and said, "Come to my office this morning and I will give you the money." That afternoon, she had three thousand dollars to her credit in the bank, and wrote checks as rapidly as her excitement would permit.

> "I do everything with a sense of reliance upon
> the Law of Good; therefore, I know that my word
> shall not return unto me void."
>
> —Ernest Holmes

If one asks for success and prepares for failure, he will get the situation he has prepared for. For example: A man came to me asking me to speak the word that a certain debt would be wiped out.

I found he spent his time planning what he would say to the man when he did not pay his bill, thereby neutralizing my words. He should have seen himself paying the debt.

We have a wonderful illustration of this in the bible, relating to the three kings who were in the desert, without water for their men and horses. They consulted the prophet Elisha, who gave them this astonishing message:

"Thus saith the Lord—Ye shall not see wind, neither shall ye see rain, yet make this valley full of ditches."

Man must prepare for the thing he has asked for, *when there isn't the slightest sign of it in sight.*

For example: A woman found it necessary to look for an apartment during the year when there was a great shortage of apartments in New York. It was considered almost an impossibility, and her friends were sorry for her and said, "Isn't it too bad, you'll have to store your furniture and live in a hotel." She replied, *"You needn't feel sorry for me, I'm a superman, and I'll get an apartment."*

She spoke the words: *"Infinite Spirit, open the way for the right apartment."* She knew there was a supply for every demand, and that she was "unconditioned," working on the spiritual plane, and that "one with God is a majority."

She had contemplated buying new blankets, when the "tempter," the adverse thought or reasoning mind, suggested, "Don't buy the blankets, perhaps, after all, you won't get an apartment and you will have no use for them." She promptly replied (to herself): "I'll dig my ditches by buying the blankets!" So she prepared for the apartment—acted as though she already had it.

> "There are only two ways to live your life. One is as though nothing is a miracle. The other is as though everything is a miracle."
>
> —Albert Einstein

She found one in a miraculous way, and it was given to her although there were over *two hundred other applicants*.

The blankets showed active faith.

It is needless to say that the ditches dug by the three kings in the desert were filled to over-flowing. (Read, II Kings).

Getting into the spiritual swing of things is no easy matter for the average person. The adverse thoughts of doubt and fear surge from the subconscious. They are the "army of the aliens" which must be put to flight. This explains why it is so often, "darkest before the dawn."

A big demonstration is usually preceded by tormenting thoughts.

Having made a statement of high spiritual truth one challenges the old beliefs in the subconscious, and "error is exposed" to be put out.

This is the time when one must make his affirmations of truth repeatedly, and rejoice and give thanks that he has already received, "Before ye call I shall answer." This means that "every good and perfect gift" is already man's awaiting his recognition.

Man can only receive what he sees himself receiving.

The children of Israel were told that they could have all the land they could see. This is true of every man. He has only the land within his own mental vision. Every great work, every big accomplishment, has been brought into manifestation through holding to the vision, and often just before the big achievement, comes apparent failure and discouragement.

The children of Israel when they reached the "Promised Land," were afraid to go in, for they said it was filled with giants who made them feel like grasshoppers. "And there we saw the giants and we were in our own sight as grasshoppers." This is almost every man's experience.

However, the one who knows spiritual law, is undisturbed by appearance, and rejoices while he is "yet in captivity." That is, he holds to his vision and gives thanks that the end is accomplished, he has received.

Jesus Christ gave a wonderful example of this. He said to his disciples: "Say not ye, there are yet four months and then cometh the harvest? Behold, I say unto you, lift up your eyes and look on the fields; for they are ripe already to harvest." His clear vision pierced the "world of matter" and he saw clearly the fourth dimensional world, things as they really are, perfect and complete in Divine Mind. So man must ever hold the vision of his journey's end and demand the manifestation of that which he has already received. It may be his perfect, health, love, supply, self-expression, home or friends.

"You cannot outgive God."

—Ralph Waldo Emerson

. . . .

They are all finished and perfect ideas registered in Divine Mind (man's own superconscious mind) and must come through him, not to him. For example: A man came to me asking for treatments for success. It was imperative that he raise, within a certain time, fifty-thousand dollars for his business. The time limit was almost up, when he came to me in despair. No one wanted to invest in his enterprise, and the bank had flatly refused a loan. I replied: "I suppose you lost your temper while at the bank, therefore your power. You can control any situation if you first control yourself." "Go back to the bank," I added, "and I will treat." My treatment was: "You are identified in love with the spirit of everyone connected with the bank. Let the divine idea come out of this situation." He replied, "Woman, you are talking about an impossibility. Tomorrow is Saturday; the bank closes at twelve, and my train won't get me there until ten, and the time limit is up tomorrow, and anyway they won't do it. It's too late." I replied, "God doesn't need any time and is never too late. With Him all things are possible." I added, "I don't know anything about business, but I know all about God." He replied: "It all sounds fine when I sit here listening to you, but when I go out it's terrible." He lived in a distant city, and I did not hear from him for a week, then came a letter. It read: "You were right. I raised the money, and will never again doubt the truth of all that you told me."

> "The universe will reward you for taking risks on
> its behalf."
>
> —Shakti Gawain

I saw him a few weeks later, and I said, "What happened? You evidently had plenty of time, after all." He replied, "My train was late, and I got there just fifteen minutes to twelve. I walked into the bank quietly and said, 'I have come for the loan,' and they gave it to me without a question."

It was the last fifteen minutes of the time allotted to him, and Infinite Spirit was not too late. In this instance the man could never have demonstrated alone. He needed someone to help him hold to the vision. This is what one man can do for another.

Jesus Christ knew the truth of this when he said: "If two of you shall agree on earth as touching anything that they shall ask, it shall be done for them of my Father which is in heaven." One gets too close to his own affairs and becomes doubtful and fearful.

The friend or "healer" sees clearly the success, health, or prosperity, and never wavers, because he is not close to the situation.

It is much easier to "demonstrate" for someone else than for one's self, so a person should not hesitate to ask for help, if he feels himself wavering.

A keen observer of life once said, "no man can fail, if some one person sees him successful." Such is the power of the vision, and many a great man owed his success to a wife, or sister, or a friend who "believed in him" and held without wavering to the perfect pattern!

REFLECT ·

1. "Man must prepare for the thing he has asked for, *when there isn't the slightest sign of it in sight.*" (p. 14)

   2 Kings in the Bible encourages us to "dig the ditches." What does this mean to you? How can you dig ditches in your life?

2. "A big demonstration is usually preceded by tormenting thoughts." (p. 15)

   Have you experienced tormenting thoughts? How do those thoughts make you feel? Can you reframe them as a sign that a big demonstration is on the way?

3. "I told her God was her supply, and that there is a supply for every demand." (p. 11)

   Have you ever thought that something other than God (or life) was the supply for your good, such as your job, or a family member, or a monthly payment? Can you now see that those are merely the channels, and not the source of your supply?

TAKE YOUR TURN ·

1. Refer to your answer to the first question above, and choose one ditch you can begin digging to prepare for the rain of good that is coming your way. Remember, digging ditches means preparing for your good in advance. Start your preparations today.

2. "It is much easier to 'demonstrate' for someone else than for one's self, so a person should not hesitate to ask for help, if he feels himself wavering" (p. 18).

Make a list of people who see only the best for you, and then ask them to begin to say affirmations for your good. Choose one to three people at minimum. Make sure to say affirmations for their good as well.

3. Pick one of the affirmations or positive statements from this chapter, write it down on a small piece of paper or sticky note, and repeat it one hundred times each day for a week. Notice all the ways (big or small) your life mirrors this positive idea.

The Power of the Word

"By thy words thou shalt be justified, and by thy words thou shalt be condemned."

A person knowing the power of the word, becomes very careful of his conversation. He has only to watch the reaction of his words to know that they do "not return void." Through his spoken word, man is continually making laws for himself.

I knew a man who said, "I always miss a car. It invariably pulls out just as I arrive."

His daughter said: "I always catch a car. It's sure to come just as I get there." This occurred for years. Each had made a separate law for himself, one of failure, one of success. This is the psychology of superstitions.

"It is your Father's good pleasure to give you the kingdom."

—Luke 12:32

. . . .

The horse-shoe or rabbit's foot contains no power, but man's spoken word and belief that it will bring him good luck creates expectancy in the subconscious mind, and attracts a "lucky situation." I find however, this will not "work" when man has advanced spiritually and knows a higher law. One cannot turn back, and must put away "graven images." For example: Two men in my class had had great success in business for several months, when suddenly everything "went to smash." We tried to analyze the situation, and I found, instead of making their affirmations and looking to God for success and prosperity, they had each bought a "lucky monkey." I said: "Oh I see, you have been trusting in the lucky monkeys instead of God." "Put away the lucky monkeys and call on the law of forgiveness," for man has power to forgive or neutralize his mistakes.

They decided to throw the lucky monkeys down a coalhole, and all went well again. This does not mean, however, that one should throw away every "lucky" ornament or horse-shoe about the house, but he must recognize that the power back of it is the one and only power, God, and that the object simply gives him a feeling of expectancy.

I was with a friend, one day, who was in deep despair. In crossing the street, she picked up a horseshoe. Immediately, she was filled with joy and hope. She said God had sent her the horsehoe in order to keep up her courage.

It was indeed, at that moment, about the only thing that could have registered in her consciousness. Her hope became faith, and she ultimately made a wonderful demonstration. I wish to make the point clear that the men previously mentioned were depending on the monkeys, alone, while this woman recognized the power back of the horseshoe.

I know, in my own case, it took a long while to get out of a belief that a certain thing brought disappointment. If the thing happened, disappointment invariably followed. I found the only way I could make a change in the subconscious, was by asserting, "There are not two powers, there is only one power, God, therefore, there are no disappointments, and this thing means a happy surprise." I noticed a change at once, and happy surprises commenced coming my way.

I have a friend who said nothing could induce her to walk under a ladder. I said, "If you are afraid, you are giving in to a belief in two powers, Good and Evil, instead of one. As God is absolute, there can be no opposing power, unless man makes the false of evil for himself. To show you believe in only One Power, God, and that there is no power or reality in evil, walk under the next ladder you see." Soon after, she went to her bank. She wished to open her box in the safety-deposit vault, and there stood a ladder on her pathway. It was impossible to reach the box without passing under the ladder. She quailed with fear and turned back. She could not face the lion on her pathway. However, when she reached the street, my words rang in her ears and she decided to return and walk under it. It was a big moment in her life, for ladders had held her in bondage for years. She retraced her steps to the vault, and the ladder was no longer there! This so often happens! If one is willing to do a thing he is afraid to do, he does not have to.

It is the law of nonresistance, which is so little understood.

Someone has said that courage contains genius and magic. Face a situation fearlessly, and there is no situation to face; it falls away of its own weight.

The explanation is, that fear attracted the ladder on the woman's pathway, and fearlessness removed it.

> "Clarity brings prosperity."
>
> —Joel Fotinos

. . . .

Thus the invisible forces are ever working for man who is always "pulling the strings" himself, though he does not know it. Owing to the vibratory power of words, whatever man voices, he begins to attract. People who continually speak of disease, invariably attract it.

After man knows the truth, he cannot be too careful of his words. For example: I have a friend who often says on the 'phone, "Do come to see me and have a fine old-fashioned chat." This "old-fashioned chat" means an hour of about five hundred to a thousand destructive words, the principal topics being loss, lack, failure and sickness.

I reply: "No, I thank you. I've had enough old-fashioned chats in my life, they are too expensive, but I will be glad to have a new-fashioned chat, and talk about what we want, not what we don't want." There is an old saying that man only dares use his words for three purposes, to "heal, bless or prosper." What man says of others will be said of him, and what he wishes for another, he is wishing for himself.

> "In order to demonstrate true prosperity, you must get rid of what you do not want, to make way for what you do want."
>
> —Catherine Ponder

"Curses, like chickens, come home to roost."

If a man wishes someone "bad luck," he is sure to attract bad luck himself. If he wishes to aid someone to success, he is wishing and aiding himself to success.

The body may be renewed and transformed through the spoken word and clear vision, and disease be completely wiped out of the consciousness. The metaphysician knows that all disease has a mental correspondence, and in order to heal the body one must first "heal the soul."

The soul is the subconscious mind, and it must be "saved" from wrong thinking.

In the twenty-third psalm, we read: "He restoreth my soul." This means that the subconscious mind or soul, must be restored with the right ideas, and the "mystical marriage" is the marriage of the soul and the spirit, or the subconscious and superconscious mind.

They must be one. When the subconscious is flooded with the perfect ideas of the superconscious, God and man are one. "I and the Father are one." That is, he is one with the realm of perfect ideas; he is the man made in God's likeness and image (imagination) and is given power and dominion over all created things, his mind, body and affairs.

It is safe to say that all sickness and unhappiness come from the violation of the law of love. A new commandment I give unto you, "Love one another," and in the Game of Life, love or good-will takes every trick.

For example: A woman I know, had, for years an appearance of a terrible skin disease. The doctors told her it was incurable, and she was in despair. She was on the stage, and she feared she would soon have to give up her profession, and she had no other means of support. She, however, procured a good engagement, and on the opening night, made a great "hit." She received flattering notices from the critics, and was joyful and elated. The next day she received a notice of dismissal. A man in the cast had been jealous of her success and had caused her to be sent away. She felt hatred and resentment taking complete possession of her, and she cried out, "Oh God don't let me hate that man." That night she worked for hours "in the silence."

She said, "I soon came into a very deep silence. I seemed to be at peace with myself, with the man, and with the whole world. I continued this for two following nights, and on the third day I found I was healed completely of the skin disease!" In asking for love, or good will, she had fulfilled the law, ("for love is the fulfilling of the law") and the disease (which came from subsconscious resentment) was wiped out.

> "I would say to everyone who wishes to demonstrate prosperity: take God into partnership with you and you will demonstrate abundance."
>
> —Charles Fillmore

Continual criticism produces rheumatism, as critical, inharmonious thoughts cause unnatural deposits in the blood, which settle in the joints.

False growths are caused by jealousy, hatred, unforgiveness, fear, etc. Every disease is caused by a mind not at ease. I said once, in my class, "There is no use asking anyone 'What's the matter with you?' we might just as well say, 'Who's the matter with you?'" Unforgiveness is the most prolific cause of disease. It will harden arteries or liver, and affect the eye-sight. In its train are endless ills.

I called on a woman, one day, who said she was ill from having eaten a poisoned oyster. I replied, "Oh, no, the oyster was harmless, you poisoned the oyster. What's the matter with you?" She answered, "Oh about nineteen people." She had quarrelled with nineteen people and had become so inharmonious that she attracted the wrong oyster.

Any inharmony on the external, indicates there is mental inharmony. "As the within, so the without."

Man's only enemies are within himself. "And a man's foes shall be they of his own household." Personality is one of the last enemies to be overcome, as this planet is taking its initiation in love. It was Christ's message—"Peace on Earth, good will towards man." The enlightened man, therefore, endeavors to perfect himself upon his neighbor. His work is with himself, to send out goodwill and blessings to every man, and the marvelous thing is, that if one blesses a man he has no power to harm him.

For example: A man came to me asking to "treat" for success in business. He was selling machinery, and a rival appeared on the scene with what he proclaimed, was a better machine, and my friend feared defeat. I said, "First of all, we must wipe out all fear, and know that God protects your interest, and that the divine idea must come out of the situation. That is, the right machine will be sold, by the right man, to the right man." And I added, "Don't hold one critical thought towards that man. Bless him all day, and be willing not to sell your machine, if it isn't the divine idea." So he went to the meeting, fearless and nonresistant, and blessing the other man. He said the outcome was very remarkable. The other man's machine refused to work, and he sold his without the slightest difficulty. "But I say unto you, love your enemies, bless them that curse you, do good to them that hate you, and pray for them which spitefully use you and persecute you."

Good-will produces a great aura of protection about the one who sends it, and "No weapon that is formed against him shall prosper." In other words, love and good-will destroy the enemies with one's self, therefore, one has no enemies on the external!

"There is peace on earth for him who sends good-will to man!"

REFLECT ....

1. "If you are afraid, you are giving in to a belief in two powers, Good and Evil, instead of One" (p. 23).

   In this chapter there was a story about a woman who was afraid to walk under ladders. Do you have any superstitions? If so, what are they? Can you see how they are representing a belief in two powers, instead of just one?

2. "Any inharmony on the external, indicates there is mental inharmony" (p. 27).

   What inharmony (or disharmony) is appearing in your life? What inharmonious beliefs are behind these inharmonious experiences? How can you begin creating more positive experiences?

3. "Curses, like chickens, come home to roost" (p. 25).

   Have you wished bad luck upon anyone? If so, who? And why? Are you willing to change this attitude and wish people all good experiences instead? Do you see how wishing good will to others will bring good back to you?

TAKE YOUR TURN ....

1. "If one is willing to do a thing he is afraid to do, he does not have to" (p. 24).

   What are you afraid to do to move forward in your life? Pick one thing you are afraid to do, and be willing to do it today. You may find that you won't have to do it after all, or that you are equal to (or greater) than the thing you were afraid of!

2. Think of someone you have wished bad luck or fortune on. Now send this person positive thoughts and wishes for good fortune. Picture

this person receiving all his heart's desires. Every time this person pops up in your mind, repeat this procedure of sending him positivity. Notice how wishing others well opens your life to receiving what you wish for.

3. Pick one of the affirmations or positive statements from this chapter, write it down on a small piece of paper or sticky note, and repeat it one hundred times each day for a week. Notice all the ways (big or small) your life mirrors this positive idea.

The Law of Nonresistance

"Resist not evil. Be not overcome of evil, but overcome evil with good."

Nothing on earth can resist an absolutely nonresistant person.

The Chinese say that water is the most powerful element, because it is perfectly nonresistant. It can wear away a rock, and sweep all before it.

Jesus Christ said, "Resist not evil," for He knew in reality, there is no evil, therefore nothing to resist. Evil has come of man's "vain imagination," or a belief in two powers, good and evil.

There is an old legend, that Adam and Eve ate of "Maya the Tree of Illusion," and saw two powers instead of one power, God.

Therefore, evil is a false law man has made for himself, through psychoma or soul sleep. Soul sleep means, that man's soul has been hypnotized by the race belief (of sin, sickness and death, etc.) which is carnal or mortal thought, and his affairs have out-pictured his illusions.

We have read in a preceding chapter, that man's soul is his subconscious mind, and whatever he feels deeply, good or bad, is outpictured by that faithful servant. His body and affairs show forth what he has been picturing. The sick man has pictured sickness, the poor man, poverty, the rich man, wealth.

People often say, "why does a little child attract illness, when it is too young even to know what it means?"

I answer that children are sensitive and receptive to the thoughts of others about them, and often outpicture the fears of their parents.

I heard a metaphysician once say, "If you do not run your subconscious mind yourself, someone else will run it for you."

Mothers often, unconsciously, attract illness and disaster to their children, by continually holding them in thoughts of fear, and watching for symptoms.

For example: A friend asked a woman if her little girl had had the measles. She replied promptly, "not yet!" This implied that she was expecting the illness, and, therefore, preparing the way for what she did not want for herself and child.

However, the man who is centered and established in right thinking, the man who sends out only good-will to his fellowman, and who is without fear, cannot be *touched or influenced by the negative thoughts of others*. In fact, he could then receive only good thoughts, as he himself, sends forth only good thoughts.

Resistance is Hell, for it places man in a "state of torment."

> "I expect everything I do to prosper. I
> enthusiastically expect success."
>
> —Ernest Holmes

. . . .

A metaphysician once gave me a wonderful recipe for taking every trick in the game of life, it is the acme of nonresistance. He gave it in this way; "At one time in my life, I baptized children, and of course, they had many names. Now I no longer baptize children, but I baptize events, but *I give every event the same name*. If I have a failure I baptize it success, in the name of the Father, and of the Son, and of the Holy Ghost!"

In this, we see the great law of transmutation, founded on nonresistance. Through his spoken word, every failure was transmuted into success.

For example: A woman who required money, and who knew the spiritual law of opulence, was thrown continually in a business-way, with a man who made her feel very poor. He talked lack and limitation and she commenced to catch his poverty thoughts, so she disliked him, and blamed him for her failure. She knew in order to demonstrate her supply, she must first feel that she *had received—a feeling of opulence must precede its manifestation*.

It dawned upon her, one day, that she was resisting the situation, and seeing two powers instead of one. So she blessed the man and bapized the situation "Success"! She affirmed, "As there is only one power, God, this man is here for my good and my prosperity" (just what he did not seem to be there for). Soon after that she met, *through this man*, a woman who gave her for a service rendered, several thousand dollars, and the man moved to a distant city, and faded harmoniously from her life. Make the statement, "Every man is a golden link in the chain of my good," for all men are God in manifestation, *awaiting the opportunity given by man, himself, to serve the divine plan of his life*.

"Bless your enemy, and you rob him of his ammunition." His arrows will be transmuted into blessings.

This law is true of nations as well as individuals. Bless a nation, send love and good-will to every inhabitant, and it is robbed of its power to harm.

Man can only get the right idea of nonresistance, through spiritual understanding. My students have often said: "I don't want to be a door-mat." I reply "when you use nonresistance with wisdom, no one will ever be able to walk over you."

Another example: One day I was impatiently awaiting an important telephone call. I resisted every call that came in and made no out-going calls myself, reasoning that it might interfere with the one I was awaiting.

Instead of saying, "Divine ideas never conflict, the call will come at the right time," leaving it to Infinite Intelligence to arrange, I commenced to manage things myself—I made the battle mine, not God's and remained tense and anxious. The bell did not ring for about an hour, and I glanced at the 'phone and found the receiver had been off that length of time, and the 'phone was disconnected. My anxiety, fear and belief in interference, had brought on a total eclipse of the telephone. Realizing what I had done, I commenced blessing the situation at once; I baptized it "success," and affirmed, "I cannot lose any call that belongs to me by divine right; I am under *grace, and not under law.*"

> "God doesn't have what you need. God is what you need."
>
> —Eric Butterworth

A friend rushed out to the nearest telephone, to notify the Company to reconnect.

She entered a crowded grocery, but the proprietor left his customers and attended to the call himself. My 'phone was connected at once, and two minutes later, I received a very important call, and about an hour afterward, the one I had been awaiting.

One's ships come in over a calm sea.

So long as man resists a situation, he will have it with him. If he runs away from it, it will run after him.

For example: I repeated this to a woman one day, and she replied, "How true that is! I was unhappy at home, I disliked my mother, who was critical and domineering; so I ran away and was married—but I married my mother, for my husband was exactly like my mother, and I had the same situation to face again." "Agree with thine adversary quickly."

That means, agree that the adverse situation is good, be undisturbed by it, and it falls away of its own weight. "None of these things move me," is a wonderful affirmation.

The inharmonious situation comes from some inharmony within man himself.

When there is, in him, no emotional response to an inharmonious situation, it fades away forever, from his pathway.

So we see man's work is ever with himself.

People have said to me, "Give treatments to change my husband, or my brother." I reply, "No, I will give *treatments to change you*; when you change, your husband and your brother will change."

One of my students was in the habit of lying. I told her it was a failure method and if she lied, she would be lied to. She replied, "I don't care, I can't possibly get along without lying."

One day she was speaking on the 'phone to a man with whom she was very much in love. She turned to me and said, "I don't trust him, I know he's lying to me." I replied, "Well, you lie yourself, so someone has to lie to you, and you will be sure it will be just the person you want the truth from." Some time after that, I saw her, and she said, "I'm cured of lying."

I questioned: "What cured you?"

She replied: "I have been living with a woman who lied worse than I did!"

One is often cured of his faults by seeing them in others.

"Go confidently in the direction of your dreams. Live the life you've imagined. As you simplify your life, the laws of the universe will be simpler."
—Henry David Thoreau

. . . .

Life is a mirror, and we find only ourselves reflected in our associates.

Living in the past is a failure method and a violation of spiritual law.

Jesus Christ said, "Behold, now is the accepted time." "Now is the day of Salvation."

Lot's wife looked back and was turned into a pillar of salt.

The robbers of time are the past and the future. Man should bless the past, and forget it, if it keeps him in bondage, and bless the future, knowing it has in store for him endless joys, but live *fully in the now*.

For example: A woman came to me, complaining that she had no money with which to buy Christmas gifts. She said, "Last year was so different; I had plenty of money and gave lovely presents, and this year I have scarcely a cent."

I replied, "You will never demonstrate money while you are pathetic and live in the past. Live fully in the *now*, and *get ready to give Christmas presents*. Dig your ditches, and the money will come." She exclaimed, "I know what to do! I will buy some tinsel twine, Christmas seals and wrapping paper." I replied, "Do that, and the *presents will come and stick themselves to the Christmas seals.*"

This too, was showing financial fearlessness and faith in God, as the reasoning mind said, "Keep every cent you have, as you are not sure you will get any more."

She bought the seals, paper and twine, and a few days before Christmas, received a gift of several hundred dollars. Buying the seals and twine had impressed the subconscious with expectancy, and opened the way for the manifestation of the money. She purchased all the presents in plenty of time.

> "Who looks outside, dreams; who looks inside, wakes."
>
> —C. G. Jung

Man must live suspended in the moment.

"Look well, therefore, to this Day! Such is the salutation of the Dawn."

He must be spiritually alert, ever awaiting his leads, taking advantage of every opportunity.

One day, I said continually (silently), "Infinite Spirit, don't let me miss a trick," and something very important was told to me that evening. It is most necessary to begin the day with right words.

Make an affirmation immediately upon waking.

For example:

"Thy will be done this day! Today is a day of completion; I give thanks for this perfect day, miracle shall follow miracle and wonders shall never cease."

Make this a habit, and one will see wonders and miracles come into his life.

One morning I picked up a book and read, "Look with wonder at that which is before you!" It seemed to be my message for the day, so I repeated again and again, "Look with wonder at that which is before you."

At about noon, a large sum of money, was given me, which I had been desiring for a certain purpose.

In a following chapter, I will give affirmations that I have found most effective. However, one should never use an affirmation unless it is absolutely satisfying and convincing to his own consciousness, and often an affirmative is changed to suit different people.

For example: The following has brought success to many:

"I have a wonderful work, in a wonderful way, I give wonderful service, for wonderful pay!"

I gave the first two lines to one of my students, and she added the last two.

It made a *most powerful statement*, as there should always be perfect payment for perfect service, and a rhyme sinks easily into the subconscious. She went about singing it aloud and soon did receive wonderful work in a wonderful way, and gave wonderful service for wonderful pay.

Another student, a business man, took it, and changed the word work to business.

He repeated, "I have a wonderful business, in a wonderful way, and I give wonderful service for wonderful pay." That afternoon he made a forty-one-thousand dollar deal, though there had been no activity in his affairs for months.

Every affirmation must be carefully worded and completely "cover the ground."

For example: I knew a woman, who was in great need, and made a demand for work. She received a great deal of work, but was never paid anything. She now knows to add, "wonderful service for wonderful pay."

It is man's divine right to have plenty! More than enough!

"His barns should be full, and his cup should flow over!" This is God's idea for man, and when man breaks down the barriers of lack in his own consciousness, the Golden Age will be his, and every righteous desire of his heart fulfilled!

REFLECT . . . .

1. This chapter discusses the "spiritual law of opulence." When you think about opulence for yourself, what thoughts or feelings come to mind? Do you have anticipation or resistance? Expectancy or judgment? What does your reaction to this law tell you about yourself?

2. "One's ships come in over a calm sea" (p. 35). Does your life reflect a "calm sea" or turbulence? What are three ways you can begin to calm your mind and experience more peace starting today?

3. "Make an affirmation immediately upon waking" (p. 38). Why first thing upon waking? How will making an affirmation immediately after waking impact your day? Are you willing to do this?

TAKE YOUR TURN . . . .

1. Think of someone you have had negative feelings toward who is currently present in your life. Now, every time that person appears in your mind, say this affirmation: "Every person, including _____, is a golden link in the chain of my good."

2. Think of an adverse situation in your life. Now, every time you think of that situation, say this affirmation: "Every situation in my life brings me to my good, including _____. I call this situation good."

3. Pick one of the affirmations or positive statements from this chapter, write it down on a small piece of paper or sticky note, and repeat it one hundred times each day for a week. Notice all the ways (big or small) your life mirrors this positive idea.

The Law of Karma
and
The Law of Forgiveness

Man receives only that which he gives. The Game of Life is a game of boomerangs. Man's thoughts, deeds and words, return to him sooner or later, with astounding accuracy.

This is the law of Karma, which is Sanskrit for "Comeback." "Whatsoever a man soweth, that shall he also reap."

For example: A friend told me this story of herself, illustrating the law. She said, "I make all my Karma on my aunt, whatever I say to her, some one says to me. I am often irritable at home, and one day, said to my aunt, who was talking to me during dinner. *'No more talk, I wish to eat in peace.'*"

"The following day, I was lunching with a woman with whom I wished to make a great impression. I was talking animatedly, when she said: *'No more talk, I wish to eat in peace!'*"

> "A single day is enough to make us a little larger
> or, another time, a little smaller."
>
> —Paul Klee

. . . .

My friend is high in consciousness, so her Karma returns much more quickly than to one on the mental plane.

The more man knows, the more he is responsible for, and a person with a knowledge of Spiritual Law, which he does not practice, suffers greatly, in consequence. "The fear of the Lord (law) is the beginning of wisdom." If we read the word Lord, law, it will make many passages in the Bible much clearer.

"Vengeance is mine, I will repay, saith the Lord" (law). It is the law which takes vengeance, not God. God sees man perfect, "created in his own image," (imagination) and given "power and dominion."

This is the perfect idea of man, registered in Divine Mind, awaiting man's recognition; for man can only be what he sees himself to be, and only attain what he sees himself attaining.

"Nothing ever happens without an on-looker" is an ancient saying.

Man sees first his failure or success, his joy or sorrow, before it swings into visibility from the scenes set in his own imagination. We have observed this in the mother picturing disease for her child, or a woman seeing success for her husband.

Jesus Christ said, "And ye shall know the truth and the truth shall make you free."

So, we see freedom (from all unhappy conditions) comes through knowledge—a knowledge of Spiritual Law.

Obedience precedes authority, and the law obeys man when he obeys the law. The law of electricity must be obeyed before it becomes man's servant. When handled ignorantly, it becomes man's deadly foe. *So with the laws of Mind!*

For example: A woman with a strong personal will, wished she owned a house which belonged to an acquaintance, and she often made mental pictures of herself living in the house. In the course of time, the man died and she moved into the house. Several years afterwards, coming into the knowledge of Spiritual Law, she said to me: "Do you think I had anything to do with that man's death?" I replied: "Yes, your desire was so strong, everything made way for it, but you paid your Karmic debt. Your husband, whom you loved devotedly, died soon after, and the house was a white elephant on your hands for years."

The original owner, however, could not have been affected by her thoughts had he been positive in the truth, nor her husband, but they were both under Karmic law. The woman should have said (feeling the great desire for the house), "Infinite Intelligence, give me the right house, equally as charming as this, the house *which is mine by divine right.*"

The divine selection would have given perfect satisfaction and brought good to all. The divine pattern is the only safe pattern to work by.

Desire is a tremendous force, and must be directed in the right channels, or chaos ensues.

In demonstrating, the most important step is the *first step, to* "*ask aright.*"

Man should always demand only that which is his by *divine right*.

To go back to the illustration: Had the woman taken this attitude: "If this house, I desire, is mine, I cannot lose it, if it is not, give me its equivalent," the man might have decided to move out, harmoniously (had it been the divine selection for her) or another house would have been substituted. Anything forced into manifestation through personal will, is always "ill-got," and has "ever bad success."

Man is admonished, "My will be done not thine," and the curious thing is, man always gets just what he desires when he does relinquish personal will, thereby enabling Infinite Intelligence to work through him.

"Stand ye still and see the salvation of the Lord" (law).

For example: A woman came to me in great distress. Her daughter had determined to take a very hazardous trip, and the mother was filled with fear.

She said she had used every argument, had pointed out the dangers to be encountered, and forbidden her to go, but the daughter became more and more rebellious and determined. I said to the mother, "You are forcing your personal will upon your daughter, which you have no right to do, and your fear of the trip is only attracting it, for man attracts what he fears." I added, "Let go, and take your mental hands off; *put it in God's Hands, and use this statement:*" "I put this situation in the hands of Infinite Love and Wisdom; if this trip is the Divine plan, I bless it and no longer resist, but if it is not divinely planned, I give thanks that it is now dissolved and dissipated." A day or two after that, her daughter said to her, "Mother, I have given up the trip," and the situation returned to its "native nothingness."

> "You are not the past. You are the present
> *becoming* the future."
>
> —Raymond Charles Barker

It is learning to "stand still," which seems so difficult for man. I will deal more fully with this law in the chapter on nonresistance.

I will give another example of sowing and reaping, which came in the most curious way.

A woman came to me saying, she had received a counterfeit twenty-dollar bill, given to her at the bank. She was much disturbed, for, she said, "The people at the bank will never acknowledge their mistake."

I replied, "Let us analyze the situation and find out why you attracted it." She thought a few moments and exclaimed: "I know it, I sent a friend a lot of stagemoney, just for a joke." So the law had sent her some stagemoney, for it doesn't know anything about jokes.

I said, "Now we will call on the law of forgiveness, and neutralize the situation."

Christianity is founded upon the law of forgiveness—Christ has redeemed us from the curse of the Karmic law, and the Christ within each man is his Redeemer and Salvation from all inharmonious conditions.

So I said: "Infinite Spirit, we call on the law of forgiveness and give thanks that she is under grace and not under law, and cannot lose this twenty dollars which is hers by divine right."

"Now," I said, "Go back to the bank and tell them, fearlessly, that it was given you, there by mistake."

She obeyed, and to her surprise, they apologized and gave her another bill, treating her most courteously.

So knowledge of the Law gives man power to "rub out his mistakes." Man cannot force the external to be what he is not.

If he desires riches, he must be rich first in consciousness.

For example: A woman came to me asking treatment for prosperity. She did not take much interest in her household affairs, and her home was in great disorder.

I said to her, "If you wish to be rich, you must be orderly. All men with great wealth are orderly—and order is heaven's first law." I added, "You will never become rich with a burnt match in the pincushion."

She had a good sense of humor and commenced immediately, putting her house in order. She rearranged furniture, straightened out bureau drawers, cleaned rugs, and soon made a big financial demonstration—a gift from a relative. The woman, herself, became made over, and keeps herself keyed-up financially, by being ever watchful of the *external and expecting prosperity, knowing God is her supply.*

Many people are in ignorance of the fact that gifts and things are investments, and that hoarding and saving invariably lead to loss.

"There is that scattereth and yet increaseth; and there is that withholdeth more than is meet, but it tendeth to poverty."

For example: I knew a man who wanted to buy a fur-lined overcoat. He and his wife went to various shops, but there was none he wanted. He said they were all too cheap-looking. At last, he was shown one, the salesman said was valued at a thousand dollars, but which the manager would sell him for five-hundred dollars, as it was late in the season.

His financial possessions amounted to about seven hundred dollars. The reasoning mind would have said, "You can't afford to spend nearly all you have on a coat," but he was very intuitive and never reasoned.

He turned to his wife and said, "If I get this coat, I'll make a ton of money!" So his wife consented, weakly.

About a month later, he received a ten-thousand-dollar commission. The coat made him feel so rich, it linked him with success and prosperity; without the coat, he would not have received the commission. It was an investment paying large dividends!

> "I do not believe . . . I know."
>
> —Carl Jung

If man ignores these leadings to spend or to give, the same amount of money will go in an uninteresting or unhappy way.

For example: A woman told me, on Thanksgiving Day, she informed her family that they could not afford a Thanksgiving dinner. She had the money, but decided to save it.

A few days later, someone entered her room and took from the bureau drawer the exact amount the dinner would have cost.

The law always stands back of the man who spends fearlessly, with wisdom.

For example: One of my students was shopping with her little nephew. The child clamored for a toy, which she told him she could not afford to buy.

She realized suddenly that she was seeking lack, and not recognizing God as her supply!

So she bought the toy, and on her way home, *picked up, in the street, the exact amount of money she had paid for it.*

> "Nothing great was ever achieved without enthusiasm."
>
> —Ralph Waldo Emerson

Man's supply is inexhaustible and unfailing when fully trusted, but faith or trust must precede the demonstration. "According to your faith be it unto you." "Faith is the substance of things hoped for, the evidence of things not seen"—for faith holds the vision steady, and the adverse pictures are dissolved and dissipated, and "in due season we shall reap, if we faint not."

Jesus Christ brought the good news (the gospel) that there was a higher law than the law of Karma—and that that law transcends the law of Karma. It is the law of grace, or forgiveness. It is the law which *frees man from the law of cause and effect—the law of consequence. "Under grace, and not under law."*

We are told that on this plane, man reaps where he has not sown; the gifts of God are simply poured out upon him. "All that the Kingdom affords is his." This continued state of bliss awaits the man who has overcome the race (or world) thought.

In the world thought there is tribulation, but Jesus Christ said: "Be of good cheer; I have overcome the world."

The world thought is that of sin, sickness and death. He saw their absolute unreality and said sickness and sorrow shall pass away and death itself, the last enemy, be overcome.

We know now, from a scientific standpoint, that death could be overcome by stamping the subconscious mind with the conviction of eternal youth and eternal life.

The subconscious, being simply power without direction, *carries out orders without questioning*.

Working under the direction of the superconscious (the Christ or God within man) the "resurrection of the body" would be accomplished.

Man would no longer throw off his body in death, it would be transformed into the "body electric," sung by Walt Whitman, for Christianity is founded upon the forgiveness of sins and "an empty tomb."

REFLECT . . . .

1. How is the law of Karma like a boomerang? How have you seen Karma at work in your life? Can you connect the dots between experiences you have boomeranging from actions or beliefs you have? What law is higher than the law of Karma?

2. We attract more of what we fear. What have you been fearing? And does the fearing cause more of it to be present in your mind and in your life?

3. What is the law of forgiveness, and how does it work?

TAKE YOUR TURN . . . .

1. "If you wish to be rich, you must be orderly. All men with great wealth are orderly—and order is heaven's first law" (p. 48). Look at the areas of your house and your life that are disorderly. Today, begin bringing order into each of these areas. Clean a closet or drawer; catch up on bills and emails; get rid of what no longer fits or serves you. Clean the rooms in your home, and clean the thoughts in your mind.

2. Make a list of people you need to forgive. Write a letter to God, calling upon the law of forgiveness for each of these people, and for yourself. Give thanks in this letter that you are under grace and not under law, and that only good can come to you and to every person on this list. You can either burn this letter safely, or tuck it away in your journal to remind you of the law of forgiveness.

3. Pick one of the affirmations or positive statements from this chapter, write it down on a small piece of paper or sticky note, and repeat it one hundred times each day for a week. Notice all the ways (big or small) your life mirrors this positive idea.

Casting the Burden
Impressing the Subconscious

W hen man knows his own powers and the workings of his mind, his great desire is to find an easy and quick way to impress the subconscious with good, for simply an intellectual knowledge of the Truth will not bring results.

In my own case, I found the easiest way is in "casting the burden."

A metaphysician once explained it in this manner. He said, "The only thing which gives anything weight in nature, is the law of gravitation, and if a boulder could be taken high above the planet, there would be no weight in that boulder; and that is what Jesus Christ meant when he said: "My yoke is easy and my burden is light."

He had overcome the world vibration, and functioned in the fourth dimensional realm, where there is only perfection, completion, life and joy.

He said: "Come to me all ye that are labor and are heavy laden, and I will give you rest." "Take my yoke upon you, for my yoke is easy and my burden is light."

We are also told in the fifty-fifth Psalm, to "cast thy burden upon the Lord." Many passages in the Bible state that the *battle is God's* not man's and that man is always to *"stand still" and see the Salvation of the Lord.*

This indicates that the superconscious mind (or Christ within) is the department which fights man's battle and relieves him of burdens.

We see, therefore, that man violates law if he carries a burden, and a burden is an adverse thought or condition, and this thought or condition has its root in the subconscious.

It seems almost impossible to make any headway directing the subconscious from the conscious, or reasoning mind, as the reasoning mind (the intellect) is limited in its conceptions, and filled with doubts and fears.

How scientific it then is, to cast the burden upon the superconscious mind (or Christ within) where it is "made light," or dissolved into its "native nothingness."

For example: A woman in urgent need of money, "made light" upon the Christ within, the superconscious, with the statement, "I cast this burden of lack on the Christ (within) and I go free to have plenty!"

The belief in lack was her burden, and as she cast it upon the Superconscious with its belief of plenty, an avalanche of supply was the result.

We read, "The Christ in you the hope of glory."

Another example: One of my students had been given a new piano, and there was no room in her studio for it until she had moved out the old one. She was in a state of perplexity. She wanted to keep the old piano, but knew of no place to send it. She became desperate, as the new piano was to be sent immediately; in fact, was on its way, with no place to put it. She said it came to her to repeat, "I cast this burden on the Christ within, and I go free."

A few moments later, her 'phone rang, and a woman friend asked if she might rent her old piano, and it was moved out, a few minutes before the new one arrived.

I knew a woman, whose burden was resentment. She said, "I cast this burden of resentment on the Christ within, and I go free, to be loving, harmonious and happy." The Almighty superconscious, flooded the subconscious with love, and her whole life was changed. For years, resentment had held her in a state of torment and imprisoned her soul (the subconscious mind).

The statement should be made over and over and over, sometimes for hours at a time, silently or audibly, with quietness but determination.

I have often compared it to winding-up a victrola. We must wind ourselves up with spoken words.

I have noticed, in "casting the burden," after a little while, one seems to see clearly. It is impossible to have clear vision, while in the throes of carnal mind. Doubts and fear poison the mind and body and imagination runs riot, attracting disaster and disease.

In steadily repeating the affirmation, "I cast this burden on the Christ within, and go free," the vision clears, and with it a feeling of relief, and sooner or later comes *the manifestation of good, be it health, happiness or supply.*

One of my students once asked me to explain the "darkness before the dawn." I referred in a preceding chapter to the fact that often, before the big demonstration "everything seems to go wrong," and deep depression clouds the consciousness. It means that out of the subconscious are rising the doubts and fears of the ages. These old derelicts of the subconscious rise to the surface, *to be put out.*

It is then, that man should clap his cymbals, like Jehoshaphat, and give thanks that he is saved, even though he seems surrounded by the enemy (the situation of lack or disease). The student continued, "How long must one remain in the dark" and I replied, "until one *can see in the dark,*" and *"casting the burden enables one to see in the dark."*

In order to impress the subconscious, active faith is always essential.

"Faith without works is dead." In these chapters I have endeavored to bring out this point.

Jesus Christ showed active faith when "He commanded the multitude to sit down on the ground," before he gave thanks for the loaves and fishes.

I will give another example showing how necessary this step is. In fact, active faith is the bridge, over which man passes to his Promised Land.

Through misunderstanding, a woman had been separated from her husband, whom she loved deeply. He refused all offers of reconciliation and would not communicate with her in any way.

Coming into the knowledge of Spiritual law, she denied the appearance of separation. She made this statement: "There is no separation in Divine Mind, therefore, I cannot be separated from the love and companionship which are mine by divine right."

She showed active faith by arranging a place for him at the table every day; thereby impressing the subconscious with a picture of his *return*. Over a year passed, but she never wavered, and *one day he walked in.*

> "I have come to see that my only business is to live as though there were none but God and I in the world."
>
> —Brother Lawrence

· ·

The subconscious is often impressed through music. Music has a fourth dimensional quality and releases the soul from imprisonment. It makes wonderful things seem *possible, and easy of accomplishment!*

I have a friend who uses her victrola, daily, for this purpose. It puts her in perfect harmony and releases the imagination.

Another woman often dances while making her affirmations. The rhythm and harmony of music and motion carry her words forth with tremendous power.

The student must remember also, not to despise the "day of small things."

Invariably, before a demonstration, come "signs of land."

Before Columbus reached America, he saw birds and twigs which showed him land was near. So it is with a demonstration; but often the student mistakes it for the demonstration itself, and is disappointed.

For example: A woman had "spoken the word" for a set of dishes. Not long afterwards a friend gave her a dish which was old and cracked.

She came to me and said, "Well, I asked for a set of dishes, and all I got was a cracked plate."

I replied, "The plate was only signs of land. It shows your dishes are coming—look upon it as birds and seaweed," and not long afterwards the dishes came.

> "Everyone thinks of changing the world, but no one thinks of changing himself."
>
> —Leo Tolstoy

Continually "making-believe," impresses the subconscious. If one makes believe he is rich, and makes believe he is successful, in "due time he will reap."

Children are always "making believe," and "except ye be converted, and become as little children, ye shall not enter the Kingdom of Heaven."

For example: I know of a woman who was very poor, but no one could make her *feel poor*. She earned a small amount of money from rich friends, who constantly reminded her of her poverty, and to be careful and saving. Regardless of their admonitions, she would spend all her earnings on a hat, or make someone a gift, and be in a rapturous state of mind. Her thoughts were always centered on beautiful clothes and "rings and things," but without envying others.

She lived in the world of the wondrous, and only riches seemed real to her. Before long she married a rich man, and the rings and things became visible. I do not know whether the man was the "Divine Selection," but opulence had to manifest in her life, as she had imaged only opulence.

> "Do not wait for a change of environment *before* you act; get a change of environment by action."
> —Wallace D. Wattles

There is no peace or happiness for man, until he has erased all fear from the subconscious.

Fear is misdirected energy and must be redirected, or transmuted into Faith.

Jesus Christ said, "Why are ye fearful, O ye of little faith?" "All things are possible to him that believeth."

I am asked, so often by my students, *"How can I get rid of fear?"*

I reply, *"By walking up to the thing you are afraid of."*

"The lion takes its fierceness from your fear."

Walk up to the lion, and he will disappear; run away and he runs after you.

I have shown in previous chapters, how the lion of lack disappeared when the individual spent money fearlessly, showing faith that God was his supply and therefore, unfailing.

Many of my students have come out of the bondage of poverty, and are now bountifully supplied, through losing all fear of letting money go out. The subconscious is impressed with the truth that *God is the Giver and Gift*; therefore as one is one with the Giver, he is one with the Gift. A splendid statement is, "I now thank God the Giver for God the Gift."

Man has so long separated himself from his good and his supply, through thoughts of separation and lack, that sometimes, it takes dynamite to dislodge these false ideas from the subconscious, and the dynamite is a big situation.

We see in the foregoing illustration, how the individual was freed from his bondage by *showing fearlessness*.

Man should watch himself hourly to detect if his motive for action is fear or faith.

"Choose ye this day whom we shall serve," fear or faith.

Perhaps one's fear is of personality. Then do not avoid the people feared; be willing to meet them cheerfully, and they will either prove "golden links in the chain of one's good," or disappear harmoniously from one's pathway.

> "Life is either a daring adventure, or nothing at all."
>
> —Helen Keller

. . . .

Perhaps one's fear is of disease or germs. Then one should be fearless and undisturbed in a germ-laden situation, and he would be immune.

One can only contract germs while vibrating at the same rate as the germ, and fear drags men down to the level of the germ. Of course, the disease laden germ is the product of carnal mind, as all thought must objectify. Germs do not exist in the superconscious or Divine Mind, therefore are the product of man's "vain imagination."

"In the twinkling of an eye," man's release will come when he realizes *there is no power in evil*.

The material world will fade away, and the fourth dimensional world, the "World of the Wondrous," will swing into manifestation.

"And I saw a new heaven, and a new earth—and there shall be no more death, neither sorrow nor crying, neither shall there be any more pain; for the former things are passed away."

REFLECT

1. What does "casting the burden" mean to you? What burdens, or "adverse thoughts or conditions," are you carrying in your life? Are you willing to cast them out to God?

2. "Before Columbus reached America, he saw birds and twigs, which showed him land was near. So it is with a demonstration; but often the student mistakes it for the demonstration itself, and is disappointed" (p. 58). Do you see any signs that your good is on the way to you? If not, it may be that you haven't been clear about what you want. Further clarify your desire, and then look for signs.

3. "'Choose ye this day whom we shall serve,' fear or faith" (p. 60). How much of each day is spent in fear, and how much in faith?

TAKE YOUR TURN

1. Make a list of the ideas, conditions, and people in your life that feel like burdens. Now, look at each item on this list and say "I cast _____ to the Christ within. I let it go completely, with love. I am free." Do this for each item on the list.

2. "Faith without works is dead." What one action can you take today that would demonstrate your faith? Now, go and do it immediately.

3. Pick one of the affirmations or positive statements from this chapter, write it down on a small piece of paper or sticky note, and repeat it one hundred times each day for a week. Notice all the ways (big or small) your life mirrors this positive idea.

Love

. . . .

Every man on this planet is taking his initiation in love. "A new commandment I give unto you, that ye love one another." Ouspensky states, in "Tertium Organum," that "love is a cosmic phenomenon," and opens to man the fourth dimensional world, "The World of the Wondrous."

Real love is selfless and free from fear. It pours itself out upon the object of its affection, without demanding any return. Its joy is in the joy of giving. Love is God in manifestation, and the strongest magnetic force in the universe. Pure, unselfish love *draws to itself its own*; it does not need to seek or demand. Scarcely anyone has the faintest conception of real love. Man is selfish, tyrannical or fearful in his affections, thereby losing the thing he loves. Jealousy is the worst enemy of love, for the imagination runs riot, seeing the loved one attracted to another, and invariably these fears objectify if they are not neutralized.

> "Success is getting what you want. Happiness is wanting what you get."
>
> —Dale Carnegie

. . . .

For example: A woman came to me in deep distress. The man she loved had left her for other women, and said he never intended to marry her. She was torn with jealousy and resentment and said she hoped he would suffer as he had made her suffer; and added, "How could he leave me when I loved him so much?"

I replied, "You are not loving that man, you are hating him," and added, *"You can never receive what you have never given. Give a perfect love and you will receive a perfect love.* Perfect yourself on this man. Give him a perfect, *unselfish* love, demanding nothing in return, do not criticise or condemn, and *bless him wherever he is."*

She replied, "No, I won't bless him unless I know where he is!"

"Well," I said, "that is not real love."

"When you *send out real love*, real love will return to you, either from this man or his equivalent, for if this man is not the divine selection, you will not want him. As you are one with God, you are one with the love which belongs to you by divine right."

Several months passed, and matters remained about the same, but she was working conscientiously with herself. I said, "When you are no longer disturbed by his cruelty, he will cease to be cruel, as you are attracting it through your own emotions."

Then I told her of a brotherhood in India, who never said, "Good morning" to each other. They used these words: *"I salute the Divinity in you."* They saluted the divinity in every man, and in the wild animals in the jungle, and they were never harmed, for they *saw only God in every* living thing. I said, "Salute the divinity in this man, and say, 'I see your divine self only. I see you as God sees you, perfect, made in His image and likeness.'"

She found she was becoming more poised, and gradually losing her resentment. He was a Captain, and she always called him "The Cap."

One day, she said, suddenly, *"God bless the Cap wherever he is."*

I replied: "Now, that is real love, and when you have become a 'complete circle,' and are no longer disturbed by the situation, you will have his love, or attract its equivalent."

I was moving at this time, and did not have a telephone, so was out of touch with her for a few weeks, when one morning I received a letter saying, "We are married."

> **"You can render to God and humanity no greater service than to make the most of yourself."**
> **—Wallace D. Wattles**

At the earliest opportunity, I paid her a call. My first words were, "What happened?"

"Oh," she exclaimed, "a miracle! One day I woke up and all suffering had ceased. I saw him that evening and he asked me to marry him. We were married in about a week, and I have never seen a more devoted man."

There is an old saying: *"No man is your enemy, no man is your friend, every man is your teacher."*

So one should become impersonal and learn what each man has to teach him, and soon he would learn his lessons and be free.

The woman's lover was teaching her selfless love, which every man, sooner or later, must learn.

Suffering is not necessary for man's development; it is the result of violation of spiritual law, but few people seem able to rouse themselves from their "soul sleep" without it. When people are happy, they usually become selfish, and automatically the law of Karma is set in action. Man often suffers loss through lack of appreciation.

I knew a woman who had a very nice husband, but she said often, "I don't care anything about being married, but that is nothing against my husband. I'm simply not interested in married life."

She had other interests, and scarcely remembered she had a husband. She only thought of him when she saw him. One day her husband told her he was in love with another woman, and left. She came to me in distress and resentment.

I replied, "It is exactly what you spoke the word for. You said you didn't care anything about being married, so the subconscious worked to get you unmarried."

She said, "Oh yes, I see. People get what they want, and then feel very much hurt."

She soon became in perfect harmony with the situation, and knew they were both much happier apart.

When a woman becomes indifferent or critical, and ceases to be an inspiration to her husband, he misses the stimulus of their early relationship and is restless and unhappy.

A man came to me dejected, miserable and poor. His wife was interested in the "Science of Numbers," and had had him read. It seems the report was not very favorable, for he said, "My wife says I'll never amount to anything because I am a two."

I replied, "I don't care what your number is, you are a perfect idea in divine mind, and we will demand the success and prosperity which are already planned for you by that Infinite Intelligence."

Within a few weeks, he had a very fine position, and a year or two later, he achieved a brilliant success as a writer. No man is a success in business unless he loves his work. The picture the artist paints for love (of his art) is his greatest work. The pot-boiler is always something to live down.

> "If we did all the things we were capable of doing, we would literally astound ourselves."
>
> —Thomas Edison

No man can attract money if he despises it. Many people are kept in poverty by saying: "Money means nothing to me, and I have a contempt for people who have it."

This is the reason so many artists are poor. Their contempt for money separates them from it.

I remember hearing one artist say of another, "He's no good as an artist, he has money in the bank."

This attitude of mind, of course, separates man from his supply; he must be in harmony with a thing in order to attract it.

Money is God in manifestation, as freedom from want and limitation, but it must be always kept in circulation and put to right uses. Hoarding and saving react with grim vengeance.

This does not mean that man should not have houses and lots, stocks and bonds, for "the barns of the righteous man shall be full." It means man should not hoard even the principal, if an occasion arises, when money is necessary. In letting it go out fearlessly and cheerfully he opens the way for more to come in, for God is man's unfailing and inexhaustible supply.

This is the spiritual attitude towards money and the great Bank of the Universal never fails!

We see an example of hoarding in the film production of "Greed." The woman won five thousand dollars in a lottery, but would not spend it. She hoarded and saved, let her husband suffer and starve, and eventually she scrubbed floors for a living.

She loved the money itself and put it above everything, and one night she was murdered and the money taken from her.

This is an example of where "love of money is the root of all evil." Money in itself, is good and beneficial, but used for destructive purposes, hoarded and saved, or considered more important than love, brings disease and disaster, and the loss of the money itself.

Follow the path of love, and all things are added, *for God is love*, and *God is supply*; follow the path of selfishness and greed, and the supply vanishes, or man is separated from it.

For example: I knew the case of a very rich woman, who hoarded her income. She rarely gave anything away, but bought and bought and bought things for herself.

She was very fond of necklaces, and a friend once asked her how many she possessed. She replied, "Sixty-seven." She bought them and put them away, carefully wrapped in tissue paper. Had she used the necklaces it would have been quite legitimate, but she was violating "the law of use." Her closets were filled with clothes she never wore, and jewels which never saw the light.

The woman's arms were gradually becoming paralyzed from holding on to things, and eventually she was considered incapable of looking after her affairs and her wealth was handed over to others to manage.

So man, in ignorance of the law, brings about his own destruction.

All disease, all unhappiness, come from the violation of the law of love. Man's boomerangs of hate, resentment and criticism, come back laden with sickness and sorrow. Love seems almost a lost art, but the man with the knowledge of spiritual law knows it must be regained, for without it, he has "become as sounding brass and tinkling cymbals."

For example: I had a student who came to me, month after month, to clean her consciousness of resentment. After a while, she arrived at the point where she resented only one woman, but that one woman kept her busy. Little by little she became poised and harmonious, and one day, all resentment was wiped out.

She came in radiant, and exclaimed "You can't understand how I feel! The woman said something to me and instead of being furious I was loving and kind, and she apologized and was perfectly lovely to me.

"No one can understand the marvelous lightness I feel within!"

Love and good-will are invaluable in business. For example: A woman came to me, complaining of her employer. She said she was cold and critical and knew she did not want her in the position.

"Well," I replied, "Salute the Divinity in the woman and send her love."

She said "I can't; she's a marble woman."

I answered, "You remember the story of the sculptor who asked for a certain piece of marble. He was asked why he wanted it, and he replied, 'because there is an angel in the marble,' and out of it he produced a wonderful work of art."

She said, "Very well, I'll try it." A week later she came back and said, "I did what you told me to, and now the woman is very kind, and took me out in her car."

> "Here is the great secret . . . you will realize your
> ideal when you become exactly like your ideal,
> and . . . you will realize as much of your ideal
> now as you develop in yourself now."
>
> —Christian D. Larson

People are sometimes filled with remorse for having done some-one an unkindness, perhaps years ago.

If the wrong cannot be righted, its effect can be neutralized by doing some one a kindness *in the present*.

"This one thing I do, forgetting those things which are behind and reaching forth unto those things which are before."

Sorrow, regret and remorse tear down the cells of the body, and poison the atmosphere of the individual.

A woman said to me in deep sorrow, "Treat me to be happy and joyous, for my sorrow makes me so irritable with members of my family that I keep making more Karma."

I was asked to treat a woman who was mourning for her daughter. I denied all belief in loss and separation, and affirmed that God was the woman's joy, love and peace.

The woman gained her poise at once, but sent word by her son, not to treat any longer, because she was "so happy, it wasn't respect-able."

So "mortal mind" loves to hang on to its griefs and regrets.

I knew a woman who went about bragging of her troubles, so, of course, she always had something to brag about.

The old idea was if a woman did not worry about her children, she was not a good mother.

Now, we know that mother-fear is responsible for many of the diseases and accidents which come into the lives of children.

For fear pictures vividly the disease or situation feared, and these pictures objectify, if not neutralized.

Happy is the mother who can say sincerely, that she puts her child in God's hands, and *knows* therefore, that he is divinely protected.

For example: A woman awoke suddenly, in the night, feeling her brother was in great danger. Instead of giving in to her fears, she commenced making statements of Truth, saying, "Man is a perfect idea in Divine Mind, and is always in his right place, therefore, my brother is in his right place, and is divinely protected."

The next day she found that her brother had been in close proximity to an explosion in a mine, but had miraculously escaped.

So man is his brother's keeper (in thought) and every man should know that the thing he loves dwells in "the secret place of the most high, and abides under the shadow of the Almighty."

"There shall no evil befall thee, neither shall any plague come nigh thy dwelling."

"Perfect love casteth out fear. He that feareth is not made perfect in love," and "Love is the fulfilling of the Law."

REFLECT ·

1. Who in your life do you love with a "perfect, unselfish love"? Which people in your life love you with "perfect, unselfish love"? Who do you love conditionally? Whom in your life loves you unconditionally?

2. "No man is your enemy, no man is your friend, every man is your teacher" (p. 66). Whom in your life have you considered to be your enemy? What has he or she taught you?

3. "I knew a woman who went about bragging of her troubles, so, of course, she always had something to brag about" (p. 71). Think about the conversations you have throughout each day. Do you spend more time talking about your difficulties, problems, and negative people? Or about the wondrous things that happen to you each and every day? How can you spend more time in appreciation and less time complaining?

TAKE YOUR TURN ·

1. "I salute the Divinity in you" (p. 65). Today, repeat this line to each person you meet. You can say it aloud or to yourself. Notice how seeing the Divinity in each person you meet affects your experience with them.

2. "Man often suffers loss through lack of appreciation" (p. 66). Make a list of what you appreciate in your life. Note large and small items alike. Repeat this exercise as often as possible to create a life of appreciation.

3. Pick one of the affirmations or positive statements from this chapter, write it down on a small piece of paper or sticky note, and repeat it one hundred times each day for a week. Notice all the ways (big or small) your life mirrors this positive idea.

Intuition or Guidance

"In all thy ways acknowledge Him and He shall direct thy paths."

There is nothing too great of accomplishment for the man who knows the power of his word, and who follows his intuitive leads. By the word he starts in action unseen forces and can rebuild his body or remold his affairs.

It is, therefore, of the utmost importance, to choose the right words, and the student carefully selects the affirmation he wishes to catapult into the invisible.

He knows that God is his supply, that there is a supply for every demand, and that his spoken word releases this supply.

"Ask and ye shall receive."

Man must make the first move. "Draw nigh to God and He will draw nigh to you."

I have often been asked just how to make a demonstration.

I reply: "Speak the word and then do not do anything until you get a definite lead." Demand the lead, saying, "Infinite Spirit, reveal to me the way, let me know if there is anything for me to do."

The answer will come through intuition (or hunch); a chance remark from someone, or a passage in a book, etc., etc. The answers are sometimes quite startling in their exactness. For example: A woman desired a large sum of money. She spoke the words: "Infinite Spirit, open the way for my immediate supply, let all that is mine by divine right now reach me, in great avalanches of abundance." Then she added: "Give me a definite lead, let me know if there is anything for me to do."

The thought came quickly, "Give a certain friend" (who had helped her spiritually) "a hundred dollars." She told her friend, who said, "Wait and get another lead, before giving it." So she waited, and that day met a woman who said to her, "I gave someone a dollar today; it was just as much for me, as it would be for you to give someone a hundred."

This was indeed an unmistakable lead, so she knew she was right in giving the hundred dollars. It was a gift which proved a great investment, for shortly after that, a large sum of money came to her in a remarkable way.

Giving opens the way for receiving. In order to create activity in finances, one should give. Tithing or giving one-tenth of one's income, is an old Jewish custom, and is sure to bring increase. Many of the richest men in this country have been tithers, and I have never known it to fail as an investment.

The tenth-part goes forth and returns blessed and multiplied. But the gift or tithe must be given with love and cheerfulness, for "God loveth a cheerful giver." Bills should be paid cheerfully, all money should be sent forth fearlessly and with a blessing.

This attitude of mind makes man master of money. It is his to obey, and his spoken word then opens vast reservoirs of wealth.

Man, himself, limits his supply by his limited vision. Sometimes the student has a great realization of wealth, but is afraid to act.

The vision and action must go hand in hand, as in the case of the man who bought the fur-lined overcoat.

A woman came to me asking me to "speak the word" for a position. So I demanded: "Infinite Spirit, open the way for this woman's right position." Never ask for just "a position"; ask for the right position, the place already planned in Divine Mind, as it is the only one that will give satisfaction.

I then gave thanks that she had already received, and that it would manifest quickly. Very soon, she had three positions offered her, two in New York and one in Palm Beach, and she did not know which to choose. I said, "Ask for a definite lead."

The time was almost up and was still undecided, when one day, she telephoned, "When I woke up this morning, I could smell Palm Beach." She had been there before and knew its balmy fragrance.

I replied: "Well, if you can smell Palm Beach from here, it is certainly your lead." She accepted the position, and it proved a great success. Often one's lead comes at an unexpected time.

One day, I was walking down the street, when I suddenly felt a strong urge to go to a certain bakery, a block or two away.

The reasoning mind resisted, arguing, "There is nothing there that you want."

However, I had learned not to reason, so I went to the bakery, looked at everything, and there was certainly nothing there that I wanted, but coming out I encountered a woman I had thought of often, and who was in great need of the help which I could give her.

> "Better keep yourself clean and bright; you are
> the window through which you must see the
> world."
>
> —George Bernard Shaw

So often, one goes for one thing and finds another.

Intuition is a spiritual faculty and does not explain, but simply *points the way.*

A person often receives a lead during a "treatment." The idea that comes may seem quite irrelevant, but some of God's leadings are "mysterious."

In the class, one day, I was treating that each individual would receive a definite lead. A woman came to me afterwards, and said: "While you were treating, I got the hunch to take my furniture out of storage and get an apartment." The woman had come to be treated for health. I told her I knew in getting a home of her own, her health would improve, and I added, "I believe your trouble, which is a congestion, has come from having things stored away.

Congestion of things causes congestion in the body. You have violated the law of use, and your body is paying the penalty."

So I gave thanks that *"Divine order was established in her mind, body and affairs."*

People little dream of how their affairs react on the body. There is a mental correspondence for every disease. A person might receive instantaneous healing through the realization of his body being a perfect idea in Divine Mind, and, therefore, whole and perfect, but if he continues his destructive thinking, hoarding, hating, fearing, condemning, the disease will return.

Jesus Christ knew that all sickness came from sin, but admonished the leper after the healing, to go and sin no more, lest a worse thing come upon him.

So man's soul (or subconscious mind) must be washed whiter than snow, for permanent healing; and the metaphysician is always delving deep for the "correspondence."

Jesus Christ said, "Condemn not lest ye also be condemned."

"Judge not, lest ye be judged."

Many people have attracted disease and unhappiness through condemnation of others.

What man condemns in others, he attracts to himself.

For example: A friend came to me in anger and distress, because her husband had deserted her for another woman. She condemned the other woman, and said continually, "She knew he was a married man, and had no right to accept his attentions."

I replied. "Stop condemning the woman, bless her, and be through with the situation, otherwise, you are attracting the same thing to yourself."

She was deaf to my words, and a year or two later, became deeply interested in a married man, herself.

> "Old ideas will not create new conditions."
> —Raymond Charles Barker

. . . .

Man picks up a live-wire whenever he criticizes or condemns, and may expect a shock.

Indecision is a stumbling-block in many a pathway. In order to overcome it, make the statement, repeatedly, *"I am always under direct inspiration; I make right decisions, quickly."*

These words impress the subconscious, and soon one finds himself awake and alert, making his right moves without hesitation. I have found it destructive to look to the psychic plane for guidance, as it is the plane of many minds and not "The One Mind."

As man opens his mind to subjectivity, he becomes a target for destructive forces. The psychic plane is the result of man's mortal thought, and is on the "plane of opposites." He may receive either good or bad messages.

The science of numbers and the reading of horoscopes, keep man down on the mental (or mortal) plane, for they deal only with the Karmic path.

I know of a man who should have been dead, years ago, according to his horoscope, but he is alive and a leader of one of the biggest movements in this country for the uplift of humanity.

"You will become as great as your dominant aspiration. If you cherish a vision, a lofty ideal in your heart, you will realize it."

—James Allen

It takes a very strong mind to neutralize a prophecy of evil. The student should declare, "Every false prophecy shall come to naught; every plan my Father in heaven has not planned, shall be dissolved and dissipated, the divine idea now comes to pass."

However, if any good message has ever been given one, of coming happiness, or wealth, harbor and expect it, and it will manifest sooner or later, through the law of expectancy.

Man's will should be used to back the universal will. "I will that the will of God be done."

It is God's will to give every man, every righteous desire of his heart, and man's will should be used to hold the perfect vision, without wavering.

The prodigal son said: "I will arise and go to my Father."

It is, indeed, often an effort of the will to leave the husks and swine of mortal thinking. It is so much easier, for the average person, to have fear than faith; *so faith is an effort of the will.*

As man becomes spiritually awakened he recognizes that any external inharmony is the correspondence of mental inharmony. If he stumbles or falls, he may know he is stumbling or falling in consciousness.

One day, a student was walking along the street condemning someone in her thoughts. She was saying, mentally, "That woman is the most disagreeable woman on earth," when suddenly three boy scouts rushed around the corner and almost knocked her over. She did not condemn the boy scouts, but immediately called on the law of forgiveness, and "saluted the divinity" in the woman. Wisdom's ways are ways of pleasantness and all her paths are peace.

When one has made his demands upon the Universal, he must be ready for surprises. Everything may seem to be going wrong, when in reality, it is going right.

For example: A woman was told that there was no loss in divine mind, therefore, she could not lose anything which belonged to her; anything lost, would be returned, or she would receive its equivalent.

Several years previously, she had lost two thousand dollars. She had loaned the money to a relative during her lifetime, but the relative had died, leaving no mention of it in her will. The woman was resentful and angry, and as she had no written statement of the transaction, she never received the money, so she determined to deny the loss, and collect the two thousand dollars from the Bank of the Universal. She had to begin by forgiving the woman, as resentment and unforgiveness close the doors of this wonderful bank.

She made this statement, "I deny loss, there is no loss in Divine Mind, therefore, I cannot lose the two thousand dollars, which belong to me by divine right." "*As one door shuts another door opens.*"

She was living in an apartment house which was for sale; and in the lease was a clause, stating that if the house was sold, the tenants would be required to move out within ninety days.

Suddenly, the landlord broke the leases and raised the rent. Again, injustice was on her pathway, but this time she was undisturbed. She blessed the landlord, and said, "As the rent has been raised, it means that I'll be that much richer, for God is my supply."

New leases were made out for the advanced rent, but by some divine mistake, the ninety days clause had been forgotten. Soon after, the landlord had an opportunity to sell the house. On account of the mistake in the new leases, the tenants held possession for another year.

The agent offered each tenant two hundred dollars if he would vacate. Several families moved; three remained, including the woman. A month or two passed, and the agent again appeared. This time he said to the woman, "Will you break your lease for the sum of fifteen hundred dollars?" It flashed upon her, "Here comes the two thousand dollars." She remembered having said to friends in the house, "We will all act together if anything more is said about leaving." So her *lead* was to consult her friends.

These friends said: "Well, if they have offered you fifteen hundred they will certainly give two thousand." So she received a check for two thousand dollars for giving up the apartment. It was certainly a remarkable working of the law, and the apparent injustice was merely opening the way for her demonstration.

It proved that there is no loss, and when man takes his spiritual stand, he collects all that is his from this great Reservoir of Good.

"I will restore to you the years the locusts have eaten."

"The key is to have a dream that inspires us to go beyond our limits."

—Robert Kriegel

. . . .

The locusts are the doubts, fears, resentments and regrets of mortal thinking.

These adverse thoughts, alone, rob man; for "No man gives to himself but himself, and no man takes away from himself, but himself."

Man is here to prove God and "to bear witness to the truth," and he can only prove God by bringing plenty out of lack, and justice out of justice.

"Prove me now herewith, saith the Lord of hosts, if I will not open you the windows of heaven, and pour out a blessing, that there shall not be room enough to receive it."

REFLECT . . . .

1. In what ways have you felt lead or guided in your life? What does a "hunch" feel like to you? When you follow your hunches, what has happened? When you haven't followed your hunches, what has happened?

2. "The metaphysician is always delving deep for the 'correspondence'" (p. 79). All effects have a cause. Think of several situations in your life—seemingly positive or negative—and "delve deep" to find a correspondence in your beliefs, thoughts, or actions. Can you see your influence on each situation? If not, continue to delve deeper.

3. "Indecision is a stumbling-block in many a pathway" (p. 80). Are you a decisive person, or do you waver and waffle? How does creating quick, sure decisions help in life? Are you avoiding any decisions that, once made, will improve your life and help you move forward?

TAKE YOUR TURN . . . .

1. Think about what you would like to manifest in your life, and then speak this affirmation: "Speak the word and then do not do anything until you get a definite lead." Demand the lead, saying, "Infinite Spirit, reveal to me the way, let me know if there is anything for me to do." After, pay attention for any signs or hunches for positive actions from you (whether they seem to connect to your desired outcome or not).

2. "Giving opens the way for receiving. In order to create activity in finances, one should give" (p. 76). Whatever you are looking to increase in your life, find ways to give that very thing to others. If you desire more money, cheerfully and lovingly tithe one tenth of your next income—without strings or obligations—to an organization

or person you admire. Give and let go, and then notice the many ways that life flows prosperity back to you.

3. Pick one of the affirmations or positive statements from this chapter, write it down on a small piece of paper or sticky note, and repeat it one hundred times each day for a week. Notice all the ways (big or small) your life mirrors this positive idea.

Perfect Self-Expression
or
The Divine Design

> "No wind can drive my bark astray nor change the
> tide of destiny."

There is for each man, perfect self-expression. There is a place which he is to fill and no one else can fill, something which he is to do, which no one else can do; it is his destiny!

This achievement is held, a perfect idea in Divine Mind, awaiting man's recognition. As the imaging faculty is the creative faculty, it is necessary for man to see the idea, before it can manifest.

So man's highest demand is for the *Divine Design of his life*.

He may not have the faintest conception of what it is, for there is, possibly, some marvelous talent, hidden deep within him.

His demand should be: *"Infinite Spirit, open the way for the Divine Design of my life to manifest; let the genius within me now be released; let me see clearly the perfect plan."*

The perfect plan includes health, wealth, love and perfect self-expression. This is the *square of life*, which brings perfect happiness. When one has made this demand, he may find great changes taking place in his life, for nearly every man has wandered far from the Divine Design.

I know, in one woman's case, it was as though a cyclone had struck her affairs, but readjustments came quickly, and new and wonderful conditions took the place of old ones.

Perfect self-expression will never be labor; but of such absorbing interest that it will seem almost like play. The student knows, also, as man comes into the world financed by God, the *supply* needed for his perfect self-expression will be at hand.

Many a genius has struggled for years with the problem of supply, when his spoken word, and faith, would have released quickly, the necessary funds.

For example: After the class, one day, a man came to me and handed me a cent.

He said: "I have just seven cents in the world, and I'm going to give you one; for I have faith in the power of your spoken word. I want you to speak the word for my perfect self-expression and prosperity."

I "spoke the word," and did not see him again until a year later. He came in one day, successful and happy, with a roll of yellow bills in his pocket. He said, "Immediately after you spoke the word, I had a position offered me in a distant city, and am now demonstrating health, happiness and supply."

> "Faith can move mountains. Doubt can create them."
>
> —Howard Wight

A woman's perfect self-expression may be in becoming a perfect wife, a perfect mother, a perfect home-maker and not necessarily in having a public career.

Demand definite leads, and the way will be made easy and successful.

One should not visualize or force a mental picture. When he demands the Divine Design to come into his conscious mind, he will receive flashes of inspiration, and begin to see himself making some great accomplishment. This is the picture, or idea, he must hold without wavering.

The thing man seeks is seeking him—*the telephone was seeking Bell!*
Parents should never force careers and professions upon their children. With a knowledge of spiritual Truth, the Divine Plan could be spoken for, early in childhood, or prenatally.

A prenatal treatment should be: "Let the God in this child have perfect expression; let the Divine Design of his mind, body and affairs be made manifest throughout his life, throughout eternity."

God's will be done, not man's; God's pattern, not man's pattern, is the command we find running through all the scriptures, and the

Bible is a book dealing with the science of the mind. It is a book telling man how to release his soul (or subconscious mind) from bondage.

The battles described are pictures of man waging war against mortal thoughts. "A man's foes shall be they of his own household." Every man is Jehoshaphat, and every man is David, who slays Goliath (mortal thinking) with the little white stone (faith).

So man must be careful that his is not the "wicked and slothful servant" who buried his talent. There is a terrible penalty to be paid for not using one's ability.

Often fear stands between man and his perfect self-expression. Stage-fright has hampered many a genius. This may be overcome by the spoken word, or treatment. The individual then loses all self-consciousness, and feels simply that he is a channel for Infinite Intelligence to express Itself through.

He is under direct inspiration, fearless, and confident; for he feels that it is the "Father within" him who does the work.

A young boy came often to my class with his mother. He asked me to "speak the word" for his coming examinations at school.

I told him to make the statement: "I am one with Infinite Intelligence. I know everything I should know on this subject." He had an excellent knowledge of history, but was not sure of his arithmetic. I saw him afterwards, and he said: "I spoke the word for my arithmetic, and passed with the highest honors; but thought I could depend on myself for history, and got a very poor mark." Man often receives a set-back when he is "too sure of himself," which means he is trusting to his personality and not the "Father within."

Another one of my students gave me an example of this. She took an extended trip abroad one summer, visiting many countries, where she was ignorant of the languages. She was calling for guidance and protection every minute, and her affairs went smoothly and miraculously. Her luggage was never delayed nor lost! Accommodations were always ready for her at the best hotels; and she had perfect service wherever she went. She returned to New York. Knowing the language, she felt God was no longer necessary, so looked after her affairs in an ordinary manner.

Everything went wrong, her trunks delayed, amid inharmony and confusion. The student must form the habit of "practicing the Presence of God" every minute. *"In all thy ways acknowledge him"*; nothing is too small or too great.

Sometimes an insignificant incident may be the turning point in a man's life.

Robert Fulton, watching some boiling water, simmering in a tea kettle, saw a steamboat!

I have seen a student, often, keep back his demonstration, through resistance, or pointing the way.

He pins his faith to one channel only, and dictates just the way he desires the manifestation to come, which brings things to a standstill.

"My way, not your way!" is the command of Infinite Intelligence. Like all Power, be it steam or electricity, it must have a nonresistant engine or instrument to work through, and man is that engine or instrument.

Over and over again, man is told to "stand still." "Oh Judah, fear not; but to-morrow go out against them, for the Lord will be with you. You shall not need to fight this battle; set yourselves, stand ye still, and see the salvation of the Lord with you."

We see this in the incidents of the two thousand dollars coming to the woman through the landlord when she became *nonresistant* and *undisturbed*, and the woman who won the man's love "after all suffering had ceased."

> "Whether you think you can or think you can't,
> you are right."
>
> —Henry Ford

The student's goal is *Poise! Poise is Power*, for it gives God-Power a chance to rush through man, to "will and to do Its good pleasure."

Poised, he thinks clearly, and makes "right decisions quickly." "He never misses a trick."

Anger blurs the visions, poisons the blood, is the root of many diseases, and causes wrong decision leading to failure.

It has been named one of the worst "sins," as its reaction is so harmful. The student learns that in metaphysics sin has a much broader meaning than in the old teaching. "Whatsoever is not of faith is sin."

He finds that fear and worry are deadly sins. They are inverted faith, and through distorted mental pictures, bring to pass the thing he fears. His work is to drive out these enemies (from the subconscious mind). "When Man is *fearless he is finished!*" Maeterlinck says, that "Man is God afraid."

So, as we read in the previous chapters: Man can only vanquish fear by walking up to the thing he is afraid of. When Jehoshaphat and his army prepared to meet the enemy, singing "Praise the Lord, for his mercy endureth forever," they found their enemies had destroyed each other, and there was nothing to fight.

For example: A woman asked a friend to deliver a message to another friend. The woman feared to give the message, as the reasoning mind said, "Don't get mixed-up in this affair, don't give that message."

She was troubled in spirit, for she had given her promise. At last, she determined to "walk up to the lion," and call on the law of divine protection. She met the friend to whom she was to deliver the message. She opened her mouth to speak it, when her friend said, "So-and-So has left town." This made it unnecessary to give the message, as the situation depended upon the person being in town. As she was willing to do it, she was not obliged to; as she did not fear, the situation vanished.

The student often delays his demonstration through a belief in incompletion. He should make this statement:

"In Divine Mind there is only completion, therefore, my demonstration is completed. My perfect work, my perfect home, my perfect health." Whatever he demands are perfect ideas registered in Divine Mind, and must manifest, "under grace in a perfect way." He gives thanks he has already received on the invisible, and makes active preparation for receiving on the visible.

One of my students was in need of a financial demonstration. She came to me and asked why it was not completed.

I replied: "Perhaps, you are in the habit of leaving things unfinished, and the subconscious has gotten into the habit of not completing (as the without, so the within)."

She said, "You are right. I often *begin things* and never finish them.

"I'll go home and finish something I commenced weeks ago, and I know it will be symbolic of my demonstration."

She sewed assiduously, and the article was soon completed. Shortly after, the money came in a most curious manner.

Her husband was paid his salary twice that month. He told the people of their mistake, and they sent word to keep it.

"Take the first step in faith. You don't have to see the whole staircase. Just take the first step."
—Martin Luther King, Jr.

When man asks, *believing, he must receive, for God creates His own channels!*

I have been sometimes asked, "Suppose one has several talents, how is he to know which one to choose?" Demand to be shown definitely. Say: "Infinite Spirit, give me a definite lead, reveal to me my perfect self-expression, show me which talent I am to make use of now."

I have known people to suddenly enter a new line of work, and be fully equipped, with little or no training. So make the statement: *"I am fully equipped for the Divine Plan of my life,"* and be fearless in grasping opportunities.

Some people are cheerful givers, but bad receivers. They refuse gifts through pride, or some negative reason, thereby blocking their channels, and invariably find themselves eventually with little or nothing. For example: A woman who had given away a great deal of money, had a gift offered her of several thousand dollars. She refused to take it, saying she did not need it. Shortly after that, her finances were "tied up," and she found herself in debt for that amount. Man should receive gracefully the bread returning to him upon the water—freely ye have given, freely ye shall receive.

There is always the perfect balance of giving and receiving, and though man should give without thinking of returns, he violates law if he does not accept the returns which come to him; for all gifts are from God, man being merely the channel.

A thought of lack should never be held over the giver.

> "I know for sure that what we dwell on is who
> we will become."
>
> —Oprah Winfrey

For example: When the man gave me the one cent, I did not say: "Poor man, he cannot afford to give me that." I saw him rich and prosperous, with his supply pouring in. It was this thought which brought it. If one has been a bad receiver, he must become a good one, and take even a postage stamp if it is given him, and open up his channels for receiving.

The Lord loveth a cheerful receiver, as well as a cheerful giver.

I have often been asked why one man is born rich and healthy, and another poor and sick.

Where there is an effect there is always a cause; there is no such thing as chance.

This question is answered through the law of reincarnation. Man goes through many births and deaths, until he knows the truth which sets him free.

He is drawn back to the earth plane through unsatisfied desire, to pay his Karmic debts, or to "fulfill his destiny."

The man born rich and healthy has had pictures in his subconscious mind, in his past life, of health and riches; and the poor and sick man, of disease and poverty. Man manifests, on any plane, the sum total of his subconscious beliefs.

However, birth and death are man-made laws, for the "wages of sin is death"; the Adamic fall in consciousness through the belief in *two powers*. The real man, spiritual man, is birthless and deathless! He never was born and has never died—"As he was in the beginning, he is now, and ever shall be!"

So through the truth, man is set free from the law of Karma, sin and death, and manifests the man made in "His image and likeness." Man's freedom comes through fulfilling his destiny, bringing into manifestation the Divine Design of his life.

His lord will say unto him: "Well done thou good and faithful servant, thou hast been faithful over a few things, I will make thee ruler over many things (death itself); enter thou into the joy of thy Lord (eternal life)."

REFLECT ....

1. "The thing man seeks is seeking him" (p. 89).

   What are you seeking? If what you are seeking is also seeking you, what ideas do you have to let it find you? Is what you are seeking in alignment with what life wants for you?

2. Throughout the book, we are told to "stand still." What does this mean, and how can you do it?

3. "The student often delays his demonstration through a belief in incompletion" (p. 93).

   Do you procrastinate? What types of things do you leave incomplete?

TAKE YOUR TURN ....

1. The square of life includes the perfect plan for health, wealth, love, and perfect self-expression. Write down your ideal outcomes in each of these four categories. Be specific, clear, and expansive. If you are unsure, ask for divine guidance to give you specific goals.

2. "Perhaps, you are in the habit of leaving things unfinished, and the subconscious has gotten into the habit of not completing (as the without, so the within)" (p. 94).

   Make a list of everything that is unfinished in your life. Now, pick the most important of these unfinished items, and begin to finish it today. Do not delay any further. You'll create new momentum once you do.

3. Pick one of the affirmations or positive statements from this chapter, write it down on a small piece of paper or sticky note, and repeat it one hundred times each day for a week. Notice all the ways (big or small) your life mirrors this positive idea.

Denials and Affirmations

Thou shalt decree a thing, and it shall be established unto thee."

All the good that is to be made manifest in man's life is already an accomplished fact in divine mind, and is released through man's recognition, or spoken word, so he must be careful to decree that only the Divine Idea be made manifest, for often, he decrees, through his "idle words," failure or misfortune.

It is, therefore, of the utmost importance, to word one's demands correctly, as stated in a previous chapter.

If one desires a home, friend, position or any other good thing, make the demand for the "divine selection."

For example: "Infinite Spirit, open the way for my right home, my right friend, my right position. I give thanks *it now manifests under grace in a perfect way.*"

The latter part of the statement is most important. For example: I knew a woman who demanded a thousand dollars. Her daughter was injured and they received a thousand dollars indemnity, so it did not come in a "perfect way." The demand should have been worded in this way: "Infinite Spirit, I give thanks that the one thousand dollars, which is mine by divine right, is now released, and reaches me under grace, in a perfect way."

As one grows in a financial consciousness, he should demand that the enormous sums of money, which are his by divine right, reach him under grace, in perfect ways.

It is impossible for man to release more than he thinks is possible, for one is bound by the limited expectancies of the subconscious. He must enlarge his expectancies in order to receive in a larger way.

Man so often limits himself in his demands. For example: A student made the demand for six hundred dollars, by a certain date. He did receive it, but heard afterwards, that he came very near receiving a thousand dollars, but he was given just six hundred, as the result of his spoken word.

"They limited the Holy One of Israel." Wealth is a matter of consciousness. The French have a legend giving an example of this. A poor man was walking along a road when he met a traveler, who stopped him and said: "My good friend, I see you are poor. Take this gold nugget, sell it, and you will be rich all your days."

The man was overjoyed at his good fortune, and took the nugget home. He immediately found work and became so prosperous that he did not sell the nugget. Years passed, and he became a very rich man. One day he met a poor man on the road. He stopped him and said: "My good friend, I will give you this gold nugget, which, if you sell, will make you rich for life." The mendicant took the nugget, had it valued, and found it was only brass. So we see, the first man became rich through feeling rich, thinking the nugget was gold.

Every man has within himself a gold nugget; *it is his consciousness of gold, of opulence, which brings riches into his life*. In making his
demands, man begins at his *journey's end*, that is, he declares *he has
already received*. "*Before* ye call I shall answer."

Continually affirming establishes the belief in the subconscious.

It would not be necessary to make an affirmation more than
once if one had perfect faith! One should not plead or supplicate,
but give thanks repeatedly, that he has received.

"The desert shall *rejoice* and blossom as the rose." This rejoic-
ing which is yet in the desert (state of consciousness) opens the
way for release. The Lord's Prayer is in the form of command and
demand, "Give us this day our daily bread, and forgive us our debts
as we forgive our debtors," and ends in praise, "For thine is the
Kingdom and the Power and the Glory, forever. Amen." "Concerning the works of my hands, command ye me." So prayer is
command and demand, praise and thanksgiving. The student's
work is in making himself believe that "with God all things are
possible."

This is easy enough to state in the abstract, but a little more
difficult when confronted with a problem. For example: It was necessary for a woman to demonstrate a large sum of money within a
stated time. She knew she must *do something* to get a realization (for
realization is manifestation), and she demanded a "lead."

She was walking through a department store, when she saw a
very beautiful pink enamel papercutter. She felt the "pull" towards
it. The thought came. "I haven't a paper cutter good enough to
open letters containing large cheques."

So she bought the papercutter, which the reasoning mind would have called an extravagance. When she held it in her hand, she had a flash of a picture of herself opening an envelope containing a large cheque, and in a few weeks, she received the money. The pink papercutter was her bridge of active faith.

> "Create your future from your future, not your past."
>
> —Werner Erhard

Many stories are told of the power of the subconscious when directed in faith.

For example: A man was spending the night in a farmhouse. The windows of the room had been nailed down, and in the middle of the night he felt suffocated and made his way in the dark to the window. He could not open it, so he smashed the pane with his fist, drew in draughts of fine fresh air, and had a wonderful night's sleep.

The next morning, he found he had smashed the glass of a bookcase and the window had remained closed during the whole night. He had *supplied himself with oxygen, simply by his thought of oxygen.*

When a student starts out to demonstrate, he should never turn back. "Let not that man who wavers think that he shall receive anything of the Lord."

A colored student once made this wonderful statement, "When I ask the Father for anything, I puts my foot down, and I say: Father,

I'll take nothing less than I've asked for, but more!" So man should never compromise: "Having done all—Stand." This is sometimes the most difficult time of demonstrating. The temptation comes to give up, to turn back, to compromise.

"He also serves who only stands and waits."

Demonstrations often come at the eleventh hour because man then lets go, that is, stops reasoning, and Infinite Intelligence has a chance to work.

"Man's dreary desires are answered drearily, and his impatient desires, long delayed or violently fulfilled."

For example: A woman asked me why it was she was constantly losing or breaking her glasses.

We found she often said to herself and others with vexation, "I wish I could get rid of my glasses." So her impatient desire was violently fulfilled. What she should have demanded was perfect eyesight, but what she registered in the subconscious was simply the impatient desire to be rid of her glasses; so they were continually being broken or lost.

Two attitudes of mind cause loss: depreciation, as in the case of the woman who did not appreciate her husband, *or fear of loss*, which makes a picture of loss in the subconscious.

When a student is able to let go of his problem (cast his burden) he will have instantaneous manifestation.

For example: A woman was out during a very stormy day and her umbrella was blown inside-out. She was about to make a call on some people whom she had never met and she did not wish to make her first appearance with a dilapidated umbrella. She could not throw it away, as it did not belong to her. So in desperation, she exclaimed: "Oh God, you take charge of this umbrella, I don't know what to do."

A moment later, a voice behind her said: "Lady, do you want your umbrella mended?" There stood an umbrella mender.

She replied, "Indeed, I do."

The man mended the umbrella, while she went into the house to pay her call, and when she returned, she had a good umbrella. So there is always an umbrella mender at hand, on man's pathway, when one puts the umbrella (or situation) in God's Hands.

> "Success is a state of mind. If you want success,
> start thinking of yourself as a success."
>
> —Dr. Joyce Brothers

One should always follow a denial with an affirmation.

For example: I was called on the 'phone late one night to treat a man whom I had never seen. He was apparently very ill. I made the statement: "I deny this appearance of disease. It is unreal, therefore cannot register in his consciousness; this man is a perfect idea in Divine Mind, pure substance expressing perfection."

There is no time or space, in Divine Mind, therefore the word reaches instantly its destination and does not "return void." I have treated patients in Europe and have found that the result was instantaneous.

I am asked so often the difference between visualizing and visioning. Visualizing is a mental process governed by the reasoning or conscious mind; visioning is a spiritual process, governed by intuition, or the superconscious mind. The student should train his mind to receive these flashes of inspiration, and work out the "divine pictures," through definite leads. When a man can say, "I desire only that which God desires for me," his false desires fade from the consciousness, and a new set of blueprints is given him by the Master Architect, the God within. God's plan for each man transcends the limitation of the reasoning mind, and is always the square of life, containing health, wealth, love and perfect self-expression. Many a man is building for himself in imagination a bungalow when he should be building a palace.

If a student tries to force a demonstration (through the reasoning mind) he brings it to a standstill. "I will hasten it," saith the Lord. He should act only through intuition, or definite leads. "Rest in the Lord and wait patiently. Trust also in him, and he will bring it to pass."

> "You can do anything you wish to do, have anything you wish to have, be anything you wish to be."
>
> —Robert Collier

I have seen the law work in the most astonishing manner. For example: A student stated that it was necessary for her to have a hundred dollars by the following day. It was a debt of vital importance which had to be met. I "spoke the word," declaring Spirit was "never too late" and that the supply was at hand.

That evening she phoned me of the miracle. She said that the thought came to her to go to her safe-deposit box at the bank to examine some papers. She looked over the papers, and at the bottom of the box, was a new one hundred dollar bill. She was astounded, and said she knew she had never put it there, for she had gone through the papers many times. It may have been a materialization, as Jesus Christ materialized the loaves and fishes. Man will reach the stage where his "word is made flesh," or materialized, instantly. "The fields, ripe with the harvest," will manifest immediately, as in all of the miracles of Jesus Christ.

There is a tremendous power alone in the name Jesus Christ. It stands for *Truth Made Manifest*. He said, "Whatsoever ye ask the Father, in my name, he will give it to you."

The power of this name raises the student into the fourth dimension, where he is freed from all astral and psychic influences, and he becomes "unconditioned and absolute, as God Himself is unconditioned and absolute."

> "Whatever is true, whatever is honorable, whatever is just, whatever is pure, whatever is lovely, whatever is gracious . . . think about these things."
>
> —Philippians 4:8

I have seen many healings accomplished by using the words, "In the name of Jesus Christ."

Christ was both person and principle; and the Christ within each man is his Redeemer and Salvation.

The Christ within, is his own fourth dimensional self, the man made in God's image and likeness. This is the self which has never failed, never known sickness or sorrow, was never born and has never died. It is the "resurrection and the life" of each man! "No man cometh to the Father save by the Son," means, that God, the Universal, working on the place of the particular, becomes the Christ in man; and the Holy Ghost, means God-in-action. So daily, man is manifesting the Trinity of Father, Son and Holy Ghost.

Man should make an art of thinking. The Master Thinker is an artist and is careful to paint only the divine designs upon the canvas of his mind; and he paints these pictures with masterly strokes of power and decision, having perfect faith that there is no power to mar their perfection and that they shall manifest in his life the ideal made real.

All power is given man (through right thinking) to bring *his heaven* upon *his earth*, and this is the *goal of the "Game of Life."*

The simple rules are fearless faith, nonresistance and love!

May each reader be now freed from that thing which has held him in bondage through the ages, standing between him and his own, and "know the Truth which makes him free"—free to fulfill his destiny, to bring into manifestation the *"Divine Design of his life,* Health, Wealth, Love and Perfect Self-Expression." "Be ye transformed by the renewing of your mind."

Denials and Affirmations

(For Prosperity)
God is my unfailing supply, and large sums of money come to me quickly, under grace, in perfect ways.

(For Right Conditions)
Every plan my Father in heaven has not planned, shall be dissolved and dissipated, and the Divine Idea now comes to pass.

(For Right Conditions)
Only that which is true of God is true of me, for I and the Father are ONE.

(For Faith)
As I am one with God, I am one with my good, for God is both the *Giver* and the *Gift*. I cannot separate the *Giver* from the gift.

(For Right Conditions)
Divine Love now dissolves and dissipates every wrong condition in my mind, body and affairs. Divine Love is the most powerful chemical in the universe, and *dissolves everything* which is not of itself!

(For Health)
Divine Love floods my consciousness with health, and every cell in my body is filled with light.

(For the Eyesight)

My eyes are God's eyes, I see with the eyes of spirit. I see clearly the open way; there are no obstacles on my pathway. I see clearly the perfect plan.

(For Guidance)

I am divinely sensitive to my intuitive leads, and give instant obedience to Thy will.

(For the Hearing)

My ears are God's ears, I hear with the ears of spirit. I am nonresistant and am willing to be led. I hear glad tidings of great joy.

(For Right Work)

I have a perfect work
In a perfect way;
I give a perfect service
For perfect pay.

(For Freedom from all Bondage)

I cast this burden on the Christ within, and I go free!

REFLECT

1. "Man so often limits himself in his demands" (p. 100).

   In what ways do you limit yourself? Do you limit yourself in the areas of health, wealth, love, and creative expression? If so, how?

2. "When a student is able to let go of his problem (cast his burden) he will have instantaneous manifestation" (p. 103).

   What problem are you ready to let go of? What beliefs are you ready to let go of? What people (if any) are you able to release with love?

3. "Christ was both person and principle; and the Christ within each man is his Redeemer and Salvation" (p. 107).

   What is the difference between Christ the person and Christ the principle? How do you access the Christ within you?

TAKE YOUR TURN

1. Review your goals from the "Take Your Turn" exercise in the Perfect Self-Expression or The Divine Design chapter, and write positive affirmations for each goal. Say those affirmations as many times each day as you can.

2. "Man so often limits himself in his demands" (p. 100).

   Are any of your goals written in such a way that you could be limiting yourself and your potential? If there's room for clarity, adjust and expand that goal accordingly.

3. Pick one of the affirmations or positive statements from this chapter, write it down on a small piece of paper or sticky note, and repeat it one hundred times each day for a week. Notice all the ways (big or small) your life mirrors this positive idea.

Additional Affirmations

For Peace of Mind
The peace of God now permeates every part of my mind, my soul, and my body; peace is mine now.

For Financial Success
The storehouse of the heavens now pours forth its abundant riches to me, and flows to me all the financial prosperity that I need and want, right now.

For Joy
I hear the song of joy in my heart, and I allow this joy to spread into my thinking, into my feeling, and into my actions; I now see joy in everything and everyone.

For Right Relationships
I am constantly surrounded by loving friends and family; I love others for who they are without judgment or agenda, and I receive all the love that I need.

For the Perfect Spouse
Perfect love within attracts perfect love into my life now; I am in the right relationship with the right person, with love as our guide.

For Healing
My body responds to the Infinite Intelligence within; I am whole and healthy and happy. Perfect health is mine now.

For Discernment
Divine Mind is never confused; I now tap into the Divine Mind to guide me to every right person, opportunity, and experience that will continue to expand my life.

For Creative Expression
The Creative Intelligence that created my life is now creating Itself through me now; I am divinely guided and inspired to express myself creatively in every area of my life.

For Releasing Fear
I believe with dauntless faith that the all-good power of the Universe is now acting powerfully and quickly in my life, leading me to safe ground every step of my journey.

Write Your Own Affirmations

As other situations arise, you might want to create your own custom affirmations. Record those on this page for future use. (Remember, be specific, and use the present tense.)

Choosing Goals

Some people know exactly what they want in life. And some people seem to have a hard time deciding what to do. Choosing a goal doesn't have to be difficult. Whether you feel you are not sure of what goals to have in life, or you feel it is impossible to choose from the many possibilities, the answer is to pick something that is positive. If you don't yet have an idea of what you are passionate about, pick something that you at least think would be a pleasant or pleasing goal to have. You'll find that as you pursue this goal, life will show you more ideas and awaken the passion within you.

Follow these guidelines, and see what goals and dreams surface for you.

Below, make a list of your dreams, your goals, everything you want to accomplish. If you have a clear idea of what you want, list those goals below. If you don't, list the things you feel would make you happy and bring you joy. Have fun with this list. Try to make your list quickly, without overthinking it. Try to list as many things as you can in ten minutes or less, starting *now*.

Next, circle the goals that you want to be a priority. These are the goals that make you the happiest, that feel the most "you." Once you've narrowed down your list, use the spaces below to write in your top three priorities.

My Top Priorities

1. _____
2. _____
3. _____

Once you've identified your top three goals, categorize your remaining goals in order of importance.

What I'll Do Next

1. _____
2. _____
3. _____
4. _____
5. _____
6. _____

7. _____

8. _____

9. _____

10. _____

Finally, take action! Start *today* by taking one step toward each of your top priorities. For each goal you've identified, do the following:

1. Begin by writing an affirmation that supports you as you work toward fulfilling this goal.

2. Next, plan a course of action. Decide what you feel is the best first step you can take. An idea for your second step may then come to you immediately, or you may want to sit in silence for a few moments to see what "comes up." Your plan could come as a hunch, an idea, an action— whatever it is, follow this positive idea and see where it takes you.

3. Repeat this process of affirming your goal and reviewing your action plan daily.

As you continue to take steps toward your priorities, you'll notice that Life will take steps to help you. Take note when a "coincidence" happens that helps you on your journey, or good news comes "out of the blue." These are ways that Life supports you.

Creating a Game of Life
Study Group

The *Game of Life* is an ideal book to study with another person or a group. Here are some guidelines that can help not only with understanding the principles Shinn covers, but also applying them.

1. Choose your study partner(s) wisely.

   - Make sure to pick people who share the same goals as you. In other words, don't cajole or plead with someone to join the group—ask people who have the same level of commitment to exploring these ideas as you have. If all involved are excited, then you'll have a better experience.

   - Choose people who will engage in an honest and compassionate way. Avoid people who will only say what you want to hear, or what they want you to hear. Also avoid those who feel they already know everything, or are negative or judgmental in any way.

   - You can find potential study partners within your family, your group of friends, and acquaintances you don't know well but admire and would like to know better. Think of people from your church, work, neighbors, social organizations, or other groups you belong to.

2. Meet consistently.

   • Once you find the right study group, make a commitment to meet at least one hour each week. Meeting in person is preferable, but you can also have discussions over the phone or via Skype if meeting in person isn't possible.

   • Don't cancel meetings lightly. The more seriously you take this, the better your results.

3. Take turns.

   • Finally, choose people who will engage with you as much as you engage with them. It's not fun studying with someone who only talks about themselves and doesn't ask others questions.

   • If you're finding the discussions are skewing toward one or two people who talk more than the others, try giving each person a set period of time to talk about how the ideas in the book relate to their life. When the time is up, move to the next person. When one person dominates, the group experience is lessened.

4. Connect daily.

   • Connecting to another person daily will create more focus on the principles, which in turn will make you more apt to apply the principles in your life.

- Connecting can be as simple as a two-minute phone call where you take turns saying affirmations out loud, or a quick email where you each write the affirmations you are repeating that day. This short amount of time should be solely focused on applying the ideas in the book to your lives. There is always a temptation to talk about other things, but avoid the temptation and stay focused on the spiritual teaching.

- Try to connect first thing in the morning so that you begin the day focused on positivity.

5. Stay the course.

- Meet consistently until the entire book has been read. (If you study one chapter a week, you'll meet for ten weeks.) Don't give up halfway through the process.

6. Reward completion.

- At the end of studying the book, reward yourselves with a celebratory meal or toast your accomplishment.

7. Continue your study.

The lessons in *The Game of Life* are timeless. Once you've finished reading the book with your group, you might try starting over from the beginning with the same group or a different one, and seeing what new things you notice this time around. You might choose a different book by Florence Scovel Shinn—she wrote a sequel to *The Game of Life* called *Your Word Is Your Wand*. Or you could choose to expand your study of metaphysics with a new book. Here are some recommendations:

- *Multiply Your Blessings: A 90 Day Prayer Partner Experience* by August Gold & Joel Fotinos
- *The Power of Now: A Guide to Spiritual Enlightenment* by Eckhart Tolle
- *The Power of Decision: A Step-by-Step Program to Overcome Indecision and Live Without Failure Forever* by Raymond Charles Barker
- *This Thing Called You* by Ernest Holmes
- *The Power of Your Subconscious Mind* by Joseph Murphy

In closing, let me say that I admire your commitment to living your life in the best way possible. As you finish this book, make sure to look back over all the questions you've answered along the way, and the actions you've taken. Applaud yourself for taking yourself and your life seriously enough to treat it with the love and care that you have as you've read through these pages.

One more thought: Please know that while we may not have met in person, I believe in you. I believe in the power of Life to work through you, and I believe that you have everything you need to live a successful, happy, positive life. Now, go and hand a copy of this book to someone who needs it, someone you believe in. In this way, you will not only be maximizing the blessings that Life is unfolding for you, but you will be creating a more beautiful world.

Namaste.

About the Authors

FLORENCE SCOVEL SHINN (1871-1940) was an American artist and book illustrator before this book was published. After its publication in 1925 she became a popular lecturer and writer.

CHRIS GENTRY is a successful businessperson, teacher, and author. He lives in New England.

LAURA BERMAN FORTGANG is a speaker, executive coach, and author. Her books include *Living Your Best Life* and *Now What: 90 Days to a New Life* (both published by Tarcher/Penguin).

Hampton Roads Publishing Company
. . . for the evolving human spirit

Hampton Roads Publishing Company
publishes books on a variety of subjects,
including spirituality, health,
and other related topics.

For a copy of our latest trade catalog,
call (978) 465-0504 or
visit our distributor's website at
www.redwheelweiser.com.
You can also sign up for our newsletter
and special offers by going to
www.redwheelweiser.com/newsletter/.